girls gone veg

To anyone and everyone who is looking to make a difference, no matter how small.
—Toni

To my mom, who has influenced my cooking and my life in all the best ways.
—Ali

girls gone Veg

Plant-Based Recipes by Athletes, for Everyone

Toni Pressley and Ali Riley

Photography by Kathryn McCrary and Jeremy Reper

Andrews McMeel
PUBLISHING®

contents

the story of
girls gone veg

This is more than a cookbook. This is a book of possibilities.

A few years ago, we became best friends while playing professionally on the same team. It was COVID; we were heavily quarantined. So to try to bring some joy into what was a very dark time for all of us, we'd leave vegan treats on each other's doorsteps. Picture Romy and Michelle leaving each other tiny Tupperware filled to the brim with delicious cakes, pastas, and tacos. That's us.

After quarantine was lifted, we were able to start cooking together and began cooking regularly for our teammates, family, and friends. Cooking became our shared outlet off the field for expressing our creativity and simply relaxing. The pressure of being a professional athlete can push you to a breaking point at times, and for us, cooking became our therapy. It became our escape away from the stress on the field, and, at the same time, the healthy food we were making became what fueled us on the field (yes, even the Chocolate Sheet Cake, page 100).

While cooking together one day, we had the idea to write a cookbook. We wanted to create a cookbook for many reasons—from simply having a documented collection of all the recipes we had developed together to showing others how plant-based eating can be affordable, from putting vegan spins on everyday dishes to showing that being vegan doesn't have to mean a total lifestyle change. All these reasons connect to the overarching purpose we have in writing this book and in our professional careers overall: **to ignite the possibilities.**

What exactly do we mean by "possibilities"? We mean hope. We mean believing you can do and be anything. We mean believing in a world in which there can be inclusivity for all. We mean believing without a doubt in what you can become.

When we started out as professional athletes, being anything but that was unfathomable. This book in your hands means we are now officially published cookbook authors. And we're just getting started.

Thank you to all who helped turn this book from an idea into a reality. What a journey it has been. Thank you to you for taking the time to read it. We hope it brings you joy and sparks new possibilities in your life. We love you.

With love and gratitude,

Toni & Ali

Two extra things to note about this cookbook:

1. Under each recipe title you will see a note written by Toni (TP) or Ali (AR). We hope that these messages give you a little insight into each dish and why we wanted to share it with you.

2. It's important to us that as many people as possible can enjoy our recipes. While the entire cookbook is obviously meat- and dairy-free, we know nut allergies and gluten intolerance are also very common. We've included different recommendations in our headnotes for substitutions you can make in order to adapt the recipes to different dietary restrictions, and you will also see the nut-free and gluten-free recipes labeled with NF and GF, respectively.

pantry staples

We've made it a point in this book to keep things fun and simple. Most, if not all, of the ingredients we use can be found in your local supermarket or online, and you've probably come across them before. However, if you are new to the plant-based world, there are a few items that you might not be familiar with, and since we use them quite frequently, we've made you a little cheat sheet.

Aquafaba, otherwise known as chickpea juice, is the liquid that canned chickpeas sit in. It makes a fabulous whipped foam just like egg whites. Drain the starchy liquid from the chickpeas and store it in a sealed jar in the fridge for 3 to 4 days. Always smell it before using; if it smells like spoiled beans, discard it right away.

Use it to make one of our favorite cocktails (pages 133 and 134).

Cashew Cream comes in handy whenever you need a sauce or dressing base, creaminess to a dish, or anything else you dream of! You can soak or boil your cashews, but we like to boil since it is the quickest, as we don't always have a lot of time to wait for them to soak.

cashew cream
MAKES 1 CUP

3¾ cups water, divided
1 cup raw cashews
½ teaspoon kosher salt
1 clove garlic

In a medium saucepan over medium-high heat, bring 3 cups of water and the cashews to a boil for 2 minutes. Then decrease the heat to medium, cover with a lid, and let the cashews continue to boil for 30 minutes or until tender. Using a strainer, drain the cashews and rinse them with cold water. Add them to a blender with the remaining ¾ cup of water, salt, and garlic. Blend for 30 seconds to 1 minute or until the texture is creamy.

note
Add more water, 1 tablespoon at a time, as needed, if the cream is too thick.

Canned coconut milk is an ingredient found in many Asian recipes. It is creamy and rich, with a smooth, mild coconut flavor. It is *not* the same as the coconut milk found in a carton, which contains much more water and other additives. When you open a can of coconut milk, you will find that the contents are separated into a thick coconut cream and a milky coconut water. Unless the recipe states otherwise, simply stir or whisk the two together (it should look like heavy cream) before measuring and adding it. Leftover canned coconut milk can be stored in an airtight container in the fridge for up to 3 days.

A **flax egg** is a vegan egg substitute for baking. Ground flaxseed, otherwise known as flaxseed meal, forms a gel when water is added to it. It doesn't behave exactly like an egg, and you wouldn't want to eat it scrambled, but it works wonders as a 1:1 replacement for egg in breads, muffins, cakes, and cookies. Allergic to flax? Use chia instead. If a recipe calls for two flax eggs, simply double the amount of ingredients.

1 flax egg

1 tablespoon ground flaxseed
2½ tablespoons room-temperature water

Place the ground flaxseed and water in a small container and stir well. Refrigerate for at least 5 minutes. Stir again before using. The consistency of the flax egg should be a thick, goopy gel.

Nutritional yeast is a powdered, deactivated yeast. The name and description probably don't have you licking your lips, but this ingredient is extremely popular in vegan and vegetarian cooking due to its savory cheesy flavor. It contains B vitamins, fiber, and protein and can be sprinkled on anything from salads to popcorn or stirred into soups and sauces.

Oat flour is exactly what it sounds like: flour made from oats! Oat flour can be found in most stores, but you can also make it at home by pulsing old-fashioned oats into a fine flour using a blender or food processor. One cup of old-fashioned oats produces about 1 cup of oat flour. If you make extra flour, it should be stored in an airtight container in a cool, dark place. While oats themselves are gluten-free, they can be contaminated if they are processed in the same facility as other grains. If you are allergic or sensitive to gluten, make sure to purchase gluten-free–certified oats for your oat flour.

Oils

Avocado oil is one of our pantry staples because it has a mild flavor and high smoke point. It's heart-healthy and is our oil of choice for sautéing and roasting. It can be used interchangeably with **canola oil,** which is much cheaper and easier to find. When it comes to a finishing oil, we love the robust flavor of **extra-virgin olive oil,** especially for dressings and dips. We will drizzle it over pretty much anything. **Peanut oil** has a slightly nutty flavor and is great for high-heat cooking. It's popular in Chinese cuisine for stir-frying. We also recommend having a bottle of toasted dark **sesame oil** on hand as a finishing oil, since it adds the most amazing strong aroma and flavor to any dish.

Plant-Based Milks

There are so many different vegan milks out there, and we like to experiment with them all, but these are the milks we always have stocked in the fridge. For the most part, they are interchangeable, but sometimes we find one works particularly well for a certain recipe, due to the consistency or flavor. We will always specify which one we recommend in our recipes. **Soy milk** is probably the easiest plant-based milk to find. It has a high protein content and a creamy texture. It has a slightly beany flavor, so it's definitely an acquired taste for drinking plain, but we like it for baking and use it interchangeably with almond milk and oat milk. Some varieties can contain a lot of sugar, so look for the unsweetened products. **Unsweetened almond milk** is our go-to unless we are making a nut-free recipe. It has a slightly sweet and nutty flavor, which is even more pronounced if you use a roasted variety. We always use unsweetened almond milk, since we like to control the sweetness of our recipes. We find that **oat milk** works with pretty much everything. Smoothies, cereal, baking, cooking— even oat milk ice cream is delicious! It is one of the creamiest options and thicker than almond and soy milk. It has around 4 grams of protein per cup, which is more than almond milk but not quite as high as soy milk. Make sure to look for the gluten-free label on the carton if you want your recipe to be gluten-free.

Salt

When it comes to seasoning our recipes, we've tried to keep it simple. We like the versatility of coarse **kosher salt** for most of our cooking and baking. However, for some baking recipes that just require a pinch of salt, **table salt** is the easiest option. You will also find recipes that call for **flaky sea salt.** While this product is more expensive, we don't think that anything can compare to the crunchy burst of flavor that this type of salt provides. It is best used as a finishing salt.

Sweetener Alternatives

There are pros and cons to every sweetener, and for the most part, we try to limit our sugar consumption, natural or refined. But we also feel that sweet treats are one of the great joys of life, so of course we've included desserts in this book. Some of our recipes use good old white sugar, and some are naturally sweetened using fruit. But we also turn to maple syrup and agave syrup for an easy boost of sweetness. **Pure maple syrup** contains vitamins and minerals and a rich maple flavor, making it our favorite choice. Maple syrup comes in four varieties: golden, amber, dark, or very dark. The darker the maple syrup, the stronger the maple flavor. It's simply a question of taste, but we usually go for amber maple syrup for that classic flavor. For recipes that call for a more neutral flavor, **agave syrup** is our pick, and we like the raw version. And for both liquid sweeteners, a little goes a long way.

Tamari is a dark, savory, umami sauce made from fermented soybeans. It has a very similar flavor profile to soy sauce but is a little less salty. Most regular soy sauces contain wheat, so we use tamari in our recipes because it is gluten-free. If you aren't concerned about gluten, you can substitute soy sauce for tamari in any of our recipes.

Tofu is our favorite source of plant-based protein. Just like most meats, you wouldn't eat it without seasoning and cooking it first. Tofu takes on any flavor you add to it and can be prepared in so many ways—in this cookbook, you will find blended, crumbled, fried, and baked tofu. There's even tofu hidden in Toni's Chocolate Sheet Cake (page 100)! For blending or crumbling, we use **firm tofu,** and we don't need to worry about drying or pressing it. But if you want your tofu crispy, it's important to use **extra-firm tofu.** And since it's usually packaged immersed in water, make sure to take time to press it dry. This process is outlined in detail for the Crispy Tofu Nuggets on page 34. If you can find the **super-firm tofu** not stored in water, this is another great option. It works well if you're making our Tofu Cutlets (page 88) or any dish that requires this very firm texture.

rise

and shine

tofu scramble

SERVES 4 TO 6

Tofu is such a great egg replacer and an awesome way to get a punch of protein in the morning. I make this recipe all the time because it is super simple and keeps well in the refrigerator. It allows me to enjoy a healthy breakfast throughout the week. You can also use whatever veggies you'd like. Get creative! **TP**

1 tablespoon avocado oil

½ medium yellow onion, finely diced

½ medium green bell pepper, seeded and finely diced

2 small on-the-vine tomatoes, finely diced

1 (14-ounce) block firm tofu

½ teaspoon turmeric

1 tablespoon nutritional yeast

1 teaspoon garlic powder

1 teaspoon onion powder

1 pinch red pepper flakes, optional

1 cup roughly chopped baby spinach

Kosher salt and freshly cracked black pepper

Slices of avocado, toast, or vegan shredded cheese, for serving

In a skillet over medium heat, add the oil, onion, green bell pepper, and tomatoes. Sauté for 3 to 4 minutes, until the onion is translucent.

Crumble the tofu block into the pan (you can use your hands) and sauté for 2 minutes.

Add the turmeric, nutritional yeast, garlic powder, onion powder, and red pepper flakes, if using. Mix well. Add the spinach to the skillet and sauté for an additional 2 to 4 minutes, until slightly wilted. Season with salt and pepper to taste.

Serve with slices of avocado, toast, or vegan cheese and enjoy!

tip

If you'd like to add vegan cheese, as I do sometimes, sprinkle shredded cheese with 1 minute of sauteing left.

hemp seed waffle

MAKES 3 WAFFLES

I love to sneak little hidden treasures into recipes when I can, and that is exactly what I've done here by adding hemp seeds to this waffle. You'll never notice them, and you get the great benefits that hemp seeds have to offer! This waffle is versatile, so you can add whatever goodies you'd like as well! Whether that is fruit, chia seeds, or other spices, the possibilities are endless. **TP**

2 cups all-purpose flour

3 tablespoons light-brown sugar

4 teaspoons baking powder

½ teaspoon kosher salt

2¼ cups oat milk

2 tablespoons avocado oil

2 tablespoons room-temperature water

4 tablespoons melted vegan butter

2 teaspoons pure vanilla extract

3 tablespoons hemp seeds

Nonstick cooking spray, for greasing the waffle maker

Maple syrup and butter, for serving

In a large mixing bowl, combine the flour, sugar, baking powder, and salt.

Gently mix in the wet ingredients and hemp seeds until most of the lumps disappear from the batter. Be careful not to overmix. Set aside for 5 to 10 minutes as you warm up the waffle maker. Spray the waffle maker with nonstick cooking spray.

Pour 1 cup of waffle batter into the waffle maker and cook until done, about 2 to 3 minutes. Place the cooked waffles on a baking sheet in a 200°F oven to keep warm. Repeat until the batter is gone.

Serve with maple syrup and butter. Or even nut butter!

2 breakfast toasts

Take your breakfast game to the next level with a healthy breakfast toast. Our Sweet Potato Toast is a great substitution for bread and is a colorful and nutritious vessel for any topping. Then we have our sweet Bananas Foster Toast that tastes good enough to eat for dessert, and our smoky, savory veggie take on smoked salmon that will definitely impress your friends. Plant-based breakfast just got a lot more interesting.

bananas foster toast

SERVES 2

Bananas Foster is one of my favorite fruit-based desserts. It uses basic ingredients, but it tastes complex and looks dramatic. My breakfast version keeps the classic vanilla and cinnamon flavors, but I've let the natural sweetness of the banana speak for itself. I recommend serving with thick slices of toasted whole-grain bread. **AR**

1 large banana

½ teaspoon pure vanilla extract

¼ teaspoon ground cinnamon, plus additional for topping

2 teaspoons coconut oil

2 slices of your favorite bread

2 tablespoons almond butter

Flaky sea salt

1 tablespoon hemp hearts

Place the banana in a small bowl. Using a fork, gently mash the banana until only some lumps are present. Stir in the vanilla and cinnamon.

Heat the coconut oil in a small skillet over medium heat. Add the banana mixture to the skillet and lightly stir until bubbly. Remove the pan from the heat.

Toast the bread. Spread the almond butter evenly over the two slices of toasted bread and then spoon the banana on top. Add more cinnamon and sea salt to taste before topping with hemp hearts.

sweet potato toast

ONE SWEET POTATO MAKES ABOUT 5 PIECES OF TOAST

So many store-bought breads are full of preservatives and artificial ingredients, not to mention refined sugar. One way to avoid all of that, plus get a nice boost of the antioxidant beta-carotene, is to make toast out of sliced sweet potato. Since you can make so many toasts at the same time, this recipe is great for when I invite friends over for brunch, and everyone can add their own sweet or savory toppings, like avocado, hummus, nut butter, or jam. Leftover slices can be stored in the fridge and heated up later in the toaster. **AR**

1 large unpeeled sweet potato (the wider the better)

1 tablespoon extra-virgin olive oil

Flaky sea salt

Preheat the oven to 400°F. Place a wire rack over a large baking sheet.

Rinse the sweet potato and scrub clean. Cut off the ends. Balancing the sweet potato on one end, slice it lengthwise into ¼-inch slices.

Lightly brush both sides of each slice with olive oil and season with salt. Arrange the slices in a single layer on the wire rack. Bake for about 20 minutes, or until tender but not soft. You want to be able to pierce the sweet potato with a fork.

Serve with your favorite savory or sweet toppings. One of my favorite combos is smashed avocado with extra-virgin olive oil, crushed red pepper, and sea salt. But I never turn down a toast with cashew butter and sliced strawberries either!

Store the leftover sweet potato toast in an airtight container in the fridge. Pop into the toaster on a medium-high setting to reheat.

pancakes
pancake pro tips

❋ Oil your skillet by moistening a folded paper towel with oil and rubbing over the surface of the skillet.

❋ Make your own delicious, flavored maple syrup by mashing up fresh berries and adding to pure maple syrup. You can even do this with thawed frozen berries.

❋ Leftover pancakes can be frozen for up to 1 month! That's some serious meal prep right there.

double-chocolate protein pancakes

MAKES 8 SMALL PANCAKES

These pancakes are for our chocolate lovers. Chocolate protein powder gives the batter a mild cocoa flavor that is deliciously amplified by gooey chocolate chips in every bite. Using protein powder is an easy way to ensure that your breakfast is setting you up for the day. Protein pancakes travel well and offer a great balance of protein and carbs both before and after workouts. Be sure to check the sugar/sweetener content of your powder before deciding to add maple syrup or not, since some supplements can be quite sweet. **AR**

1 cup all-purpose flour

¼ cup chocolate-flavored vegan protein powder

2 teaspoons baking powder

Pinch of ground cinnamon

1 cup plant-based milk, plus additional as needed (I like to use unsweetened soy milk for its consistency)

1 teaspoon pure vanilla extract

1 tablespoon maple syrup, plus additional for serving

¼ cup vegan chocolate chips (we love mini chocolate chips)

Canola oil, for the skillet

Vegan butter, for serving

Preheat the oven to 200°F.

In a medium bowl, whisk together the flour, protein powder, baking powder, and cinnamon.

Add the milk, vanilla, and maple syrup, if using, and mix just until smooth. Be careful not to overmix. If the batter feels too thick, add more milk, 1 tablespoon at a time. Stir in the chocolate chips.

Heat a lightly oiled skillet over medium heat. Once the skillet is hot, use a ¼-cup measuring cup to scoop the batter onto the skillet. Cook until bubbles form and the pancake edges are dry, about 1 minute. Flip and cook the other side for about 1 minute more. Transfer to a baking dish or ovenproof platter, cover loosely with aluminum foil, and place in the oven to stay warm until serving. Repeat with the remaining batter, continuing to add more oil to the skillet between pancakes as needed.

Serve with vegan butter and maple syrup, or pack them up for the road. These will keep in the fridge in an airtight container for 3 to 4 days. Reheat in the toaster or microwave.

banana–berry buckwheat pancakes

MAKES 8 MEDIUM PANCAKES

Buckwheat flour is a grain- and gluten-free flour high in protein and fiber, with a nutty flavor. These fluffy pancakes use banana and blueberries to balance out the earthiness of the buckwheat, so they can be super healthy without tasting super healthy, if you know what I mean. **AR**

½ medium banana

⅔ cup plant-based milk (I recommend oat or almond milk)

2 teaspoons apple cider vinegar

½ teaspoon pure vanilla extract

½ teaspoon maple syrup, optional, plus additional for serving

1 cup buckwheat flour

1 teaspoon baking powder

¼ teaspoon baking soda

½ teaspoon ground cinnamon

Pinch of table salt

¾ cup fresh blueberries

Vegan butter, for serving

Preheat the oven to 200°F.

Place the banana in a medium bowl. Using a fork, gently mash the banana until no lumps remain.

Whisk in the milk, vinegar, vanilla, and maple syrup, if using. Add the buckwheat flour, baking powder, baking soda, cinnamon, and salt, and mix until smooth. Stir in the berries and allow the batter to rest for 5 minutes.

Heat a lightly oiled skillet over medium heat. Once the skillet is hot, use a ¼-cup measuring cup to scoop the batter onto the skillet. Cook until bubbles form and the pancake edges are dry, about 1 minute. Flip and cook the other side for about 1 minute more. Transfer to a baking dish or ovenproof platter, cover loosely with aluminum foil, and place in the oven to stay warm until serving. Repeat with the remaining batter, continuing to add more oil to the skillet between pancakes as needed.

Serve warm with butter and maple syrup. These will keep in the fridge in an airtight container for 3 to 4 days. Reheat pancakes in the toaster or microwave.

apple–cinnamon baked PROatmeal

SERVES 6 TO 8

Take your oatmeal game to the next level by adding protein powder and baking it in the oven. This is a perfect recipe for meal prepping your breakfasts and post-workout snacks for the week, since it makes up to 8 servings and can be stored in the fridge for up to 5 days. For breakfast, I like to heat up a bar in the microwave, to get it nice and hot, pour some cold oat milk on top, and add a splash of maple syrup. But when I'm in a rush, I just grab a bar and hit the road! **AR**

2 medium apples (I recommend Honeycrisp)

Nonstick cooking spray, for greasing the baking dish

2½ cups gluten-free old-fashioned rolled oats

⅓ cup vanilla-flavored vegan protein powder

2 teaspoons ground cinnamon

Pinch of table salt

2 cups plant-based milk (I like to use oat milk)

½ cup unsweetened applesauce

½ teaspoon pure vanilla extract

¼ cup maple syrup, optional

Additional plant-based milk and maple syrup, for serving

Preheat the oven to 350°F. Core your apples, leaving the peel on, and dice them into ½-inch cubes. Set the apples aside.

Grease an 8 by 8-inch baking dish. Place the oats, protein powder, cinnamon, and salt into the dish. Mix with a fork until combined. Add the milk, applesauce, vanilla, and maple syrup, if using. Stir to cover all the dry ingredients with the wet ingredients. Stir in the apples and pour into the prepared baking dish.

Bake for about 35 minutes, or until firm to the touch.

Serve immediately by scooping out desired portions and adding milk and syrup to your liking. Or allow the PROatmeal to cool completely before cutting it into bars. Store the bars in the refrigerator in an airtight container or resealable bag for up to 5 days. Enjoy cold or reheated in the microwave, checking on it every 15 seconds until it reaches your desired temperature.

Bircher muesli

SERVES 4

The Swiss physician Maximilian Bircher-Benner created the OG overnight oats in the early 1900s to encourage his patients to eat healthier, and I've been lucky enough to enjoy the refreshing breakfast item in both Switzerland and Germany while traveling with the New Zealand national team. Different versions use different liquids and fruits, and I like to mix up different combinations depending on the season and my mood. But I always keep the grated apple and slivered almonds for that sweetness and crunch! Remember to make these a day in advance, since they need to be refrigerated overnight. **AR**

2 cups gluten-free old-fashioned rolled oats

1 large apple, skin on, coarsely grated (I like to use Granny Smith), plus additional chopped apple, for garnish

½ cup raisins

¼ cup slivered almonds

1 teaspoon ground cinnamon

¼ teaspoon ground ginger

2½ cups plant-based milk (I like vanilla pea milk for the high protein content), plus extra for serving

Place all the ingredients into a small bowl and stir to mix. Cover and refrigerate overnight. Bircher muesli can be kept covered in the fridge for up to 4 days. When you're ready to serve, spoon into individual bowls or jars. If desired, top with a splash of milk and chopped fresh apple.

carrot lox

SERVES 2 TO 3

When I was little, my parents and I would go to the beach on Sundays with a bag of bagels, a tub of cream cheese, and some slices of smoked salmon. Eventually soccer took over the weekends, but sometimes on the way home from a game I could convince my dad to swing by our local bagel shop for my favorite breakfast. These carrots pick up the saltiness and smokiness that I've always loved, especially when sandwiched between two warm bagel halves smothered in cream cheese. Allow for 30 minutes of marinating time. **AR**

1 large, peeled carrot (the thicker the carrot, the more servings)

2 tablespoons caper brine

1 tablespoon rice vinegar

½ tablespoon avocado oil

1 teaspoon tamari

1 teaspoon maple syrup

½ teaspoon liquid smoke

½ teaspoon freshly squeezed lemon juice

Toasted bagels, vegan cream cheese, red onion slices, capers, and fresh dill, for serving

Fill a medium pot with 1 to 2 inches of water and place a steamer basket in the bottom of the pot. Bring the water to a boil over medium-high heat.

Lay the carrot flat on a cutting board. Using a vegetable peeler, slice the carrot lengthwise to create a ribbon. Repeat until the carrot is too thin to peel. Place the ribbons into the steamer basket, cover, and steam for 7 to 8 minutes, until tender.

Remove the carrots from the steamer and place them in a medium bowl. Add the caper brine, rice vinegar, oil, tamari, maple syrup, liquid smoke, and lemon juice. Toss gently to completely coat the carrots. Cover the bowl with a lid or plastic wrap and place in the fridge. Allow the carrots to marinate for at least 30 minutes, but ideally overnight.

Serve with toasted bagels, vegan cream cheese, red onion slices, capers, and fresh dill.

oatmeal-raisin breakfast cookies

MAKES 8 COOKIES

A healthy and super-portable breakfast that gives you cookie vibes while serving you fiber and protein. With very little added sugar, these are basically oatmeal in cookie form. You can easily personalize these cookies by replacing the raisins with other goodies. Dried cranberries or vegan chocolate chips will make them sweeter, and chopped nuts will give them a nice crunch. **AR**

Nonstick cooking spray, for greasing the baking sheet

1½ medium ripe bananas

1 cup gluten-free old-fashioned rolled oats

¼ cup hemp hearts

¼ cup raisins

3 tablespoons unsweetened applesauce

3 tablespoons plant-based milk (I use unsweetened vanilla oat milk)

1 tablespoon agave nectar

½ teaspoon pure vanilla extract

½ teaspoon ground cinnamon

Pinch of table salt

Preheat the oven to 350°F. Grease a small baking sheet with non-stick cooking spray.

Place the banana in a medium bowl. Using a fork, gently mash the banana until there are no lumps.

Add the remaining ingredients and mix until well combined. Drop by the spoonful onto the baking sheet and spread into circular cookie shapes. Bake for 20 minutes, or until firm to the touch. Enjoy warm, but allow to cool to room temperature before storing.

Store covered in the fridge for up to 1 week.

mom's favorite scones

Scones are a big part of New Zealand coffee and tea culture, and while I don't drink coffee or tea, I never turn down a scone. These slightly sweet scones get their delicious flavor and density from the combination of banana and almond flour, making them a lot healthier (more protein and fiber) than a traditional scone, plus they're gluten-free! My mom says she could eat them every day. These are best served warm with vegan butter and Strawberry Chia Jam (page 20). **AR**

2 large bananas

1 cup almond flour

2 tablespoons coconut flour

1 teaspoon baking powder

Pinch of table salt

2 flax eggs (page x)

Vegan chocolate chips, dried cranberries, or chopped dates, for mix-ins

Vegan butter and your favorite jam, for serving

Preheat the oven to 400°F. Line a large baking sheet with parchment paper.

Place the bananas in a medium bowl. Using a fork, gently mash the bananas until no lumps remain. Stir in the almond flour, coconut flour, baking powder, and salt. Gently fold in the flax eggs and your mix-ins, if using.

Form four large circular mounds on the lined baking sheet.

Bake for 15 to 20 minutes, or until golden brown on top and firm to the touch. Remove and allow to cool to room temperature before serving with vegan butter, jam, and your favorite cup of tea.

strawberry chia jam

MAKES 1½ CUPS

This jam recipe gives chia seeds a chance to show off their magic powers as they transform berries into a thick spread. I don't think you'll want to go back to traditional jam packed with sugars and artificial sweeteners after tasting this fiber-packed explosion of real fruit flavor. **AR**

2 cups hulled fresh strawberries, roughly chopped

1½ tablespoons freshly squeezed lemon juice

2 tablespoons chia seeds

1 tablespoon maple syrup, optional

Place your fresh strawberries in a small saucepan. Cook over medium heat, stirring occasionally. When the berries start to break down and the juices are bubbling, after about 6 to 8 minutes, use a potato masher or fork to mash them into your desired jam texture. You might not like big chunks of strawberry in your jam, or maybe you do!

Remove from the heat and stir in the lemon juice and chia seeds. Add the maple syrup, if using.

Let the jam cool for 10 minutes before eating. It will get nice and thick during this time. Spread it on toast, mix it into a plant-based yogurt, or even use it as an ice-cream topping. My favorite way to eat this jam is lathered on top of a warm, buttered scone (page 18). Once cooled completely, you can store your jam in the fridge in an airtight container for up to 1 week.

b*ite

me

artichoke spread

MAKES 1 CUP

Have you ever made something at home and thought, "I am never buying this from the store again"? Well, this is one of those recipes. This is the spread of all spreads. Put it on your sandwich, your pasta, or your pizza. Or be like Toni and just eat it with a spoon. Artichokes are one of the most antioxidant-rich vegetables out there, but fresh artichokes can be intimidating. By using canned artichoke hearts, you get the best part of the artichoke without any of the work, and you have a fancy spread in under 5 minutes. **AR**

1 (14-ounce) can quartered artichoke hearts, drained

1 clove garlic

½ cup extra-virgin olive oil, plus more for drizzling

½ teaspoon flaky sea salt, divided

Toasted baguette slices or crackers, for serving

Place the artichoke, garlic, olive oil, and ¼ teaspoon of the salt into a food processor or blender and process until smooth. Scoop into a bowl and top with a drizzle of extra-virgin olive oil and the remaining ¼ teaspoon of salt. Serve with toasted baguette slices or crackers. Store any leftover spread in a sealed container in the fridge for 3 to 4 days.

3 delectable dips

beet hummus

MAKES 2 CUPS

When I talk to people about nutrition, one of my first pieces of advice is to "eat a rainbow." Fruits and veggies give us nutrients that make us feel full longer, boost our immune system, and reduce the risk of various diseases. Different colors of fruits and veggies provide different awesome health benefits, which is why we should try to eat all the colors of the rainbow. The earthy beet, with its deep reddish-purple hue, is known to lower blood pressure, aid in digestion, and reduce inflammation. Just try not to get it on your clothes. If you don't want to spend time roasting the beet, you can buy already-cooked beets at the grocery store. The chickpea liquid can even be used for the cocktails on pages 133 and 134. **AR**

1 medium beet

¼ cup extra-virgin olive oil, plus additional for coating the beet and drizzling over the hummus

1 (15-ounce) can chickpeas, drained and rinsed

⅓ cup tahini

1 clove garlic, roughly chopped

Finely grated zest and juice of 1 lemon

½ teaspoon flaky sea salt, plus additional as needed

2 to 3 tablespoons water, as needed

Pita chips, crackers, or veggies, for serving

Preheat the oven to 400°F. Place an oven rack in the middle position.

(Skip the next step if using an already cooked beet.)

Wash the beet well, making sure to scrub off any dirt. Trim off the leaves. Coat the beet lightly with extra-virgin olive oil and wrap it in aluminum foil. Make sure the beet is completely wrapped. Place the aluminum-wrapped beet on the oven rack and roast for 40 minutes. Take out the beet, unwrap it, and pierce it with a knife. If the knife can slide to the center of the beet with no resistance, the beet is done. If not, rewrap it and continue to roast it, checking the tenderness every 10 minutes.

Once the beet is done, let it cool for five minutes. Then place it under running water and rub off the skin.

Cut the beet into quarters.

Continued

Place the beet, chickpeas, tahini, garlic, lemon zest, lemon juice, and ½ teaspoon of salt into a food processor. Blend until smooth. With the motor running, slowly add the ¼ cup of olive oil and continue to blend until combined. If the hummus is too thick, blend in water, 1 tablespoon at a time, until you reach the desired consistency. Add additional salt to taste.

Spoon into a bowl and drizzle over additional olive oil for serving. Serve with pita chips, crackers, or crunchy vegetables like carrots or celery.

Store the hummus in a sealed container in the fridge for up to 3 days.

edamame hummus

MAKES **2** CUPS

Edamame beans are a whole protein source that work perfectly in a hummus recipe. If you're a cilantro lover like us, you will love this delicious green dip. I like to make this hummus a day before serving it since it becomes even more flavorful after a night in the fridge. **AR**

1½ cups frozen shelled edamame

¼ cup tahini

1 teaspoon finely grated lemon zest

3 tablespoons freshly squeezed lemon juice

1 clove garlic

½ teaspoon flaky sea salt, plus additional as needed

¼ teaspoon ground cumin

¼ cup water

4 tablespoons extra-virgin olive oil, plus additional for drizzling

1 tablespoon finely chopped cilantro

Crackers or veggie sticks, for serving

Cook the edamame by dropping them into lightly salted boiling water for 5 minutes.

Drain the edamame before placing them in a food processor along with the tahini, lemon zest, lemon juice, garlic, salt, cumin, and water. Blend until smooth. With the motor running, slowly add the 4 tablespoons of olive oil and continue to blend until combined.

Scoop into a sealed container and refrigerate for at least 1 hour, and ideally overnight.

Just before serving, remove from the fridge, stir in the cilantro, and add salt to taste. Drizzle some additional extra-virgin olive oil over the top. Serve with your favorite crackers or veggie sticks. Store the hummus in a sealed container in the fridge for up to 3 days.

sweet potato and white bean hummus

MAKES 2 CUPS

This vibrant hummus gives you fiber, vitamins, and minerals from sweet potato *plus* a nice punch of protein from cannellini beans. Cannellini beans have a nutty flavor similar to that of chickpeas but are slightly richer in protein, making them a great substitute in a hummus recipe. **AR**

- 1 small sweet potato, peeled and cut into 1-inch cubes
- 1 (15-ounce) can cannellini beans, drained and rinsed
- 2 tablespoons tahini
- 2 cloves garlic
- Freshly squeezed juice of ½ lemon
- 1½ teaspoons kosher salt
- Extra-virgin olive oil, for drizzling
- Tortilla chips or sourdough bread slices, for serving

Bring a large pot of water to a boil. There should be enough water in the pot to cover the sweet potato by at least 1 inch. Carefully add the sweet potato cubes. Decrease the heat to medium-high and slowly boil the sweet potato until cooked through, or about 15 minutes. Drain the sweet potato in a colander.

Transfer the sweet potato to a food processor. Add the beans, tahini, garlic, lemon juice, and salt. Blend until smooth. Before serving, drizzle with some olive oil. I love serving this hummus with salty tortilla chips or sourdough bread. Store leftover hummus in a sealed container in the fridge for up to 3 to 4 days.

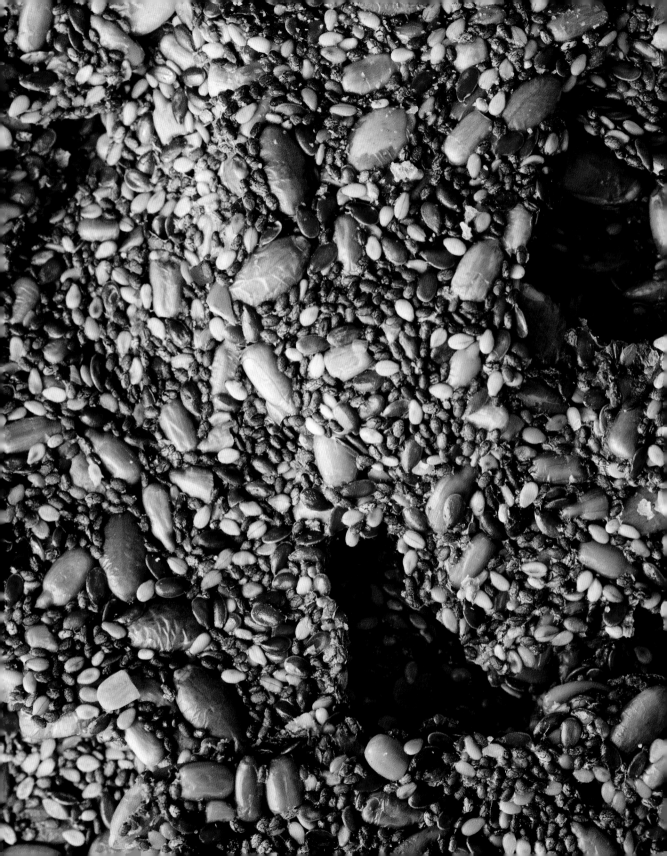

seed crackers

SERVES 4

These crispy crackers are made from seeds only, which means they are rich in nutrients and give you long-lasting energy. It's amazing how the chia seeds just soak up all the water and bind everything together while providing calcium and iron. I love using these crackers as a healthy vessel to dunk into my favorite dips, and you can personalize them with your favorite mix of 1½ cups of seeds, in addition to the ½ cup of chia seeds. **AR**

½ cup pumpkin seeds

½ cup sunflower seeds

¼ cup sesame seeds

¼ cup whole flax seeds

½ cup chia seeds

2 tablespoons extra-virgin olive oil

1 cup boiling water

Flaky sea salt

Preheat the oven to 300°F. Line a large baking sheet with parchment paper.

Place the pumpkin seeds, sunflower seeds, sesame seeds, flax seeds, chia seeds, extra-virgin olive oil, and water into a large bowl. Stir to combine. Let the mixture rest for 10 minutes. You should be left with a thick seed gel.

Pour the seed gel mixture onto the baking sheet. Place a second piece of parchment paper on top of the mixture and then use your hands or a rolling pin to spread the mixture as thin and evenly as possible. Remove the top parchment paper and sprinkle sea salt over the mixture.

Bake for 50 minutes or until the cracker sheet is dry and turning golden brown. Let it come to room temperature before breaking it into pieces of your desired cracker shape and size. Serve with one of our delectable dips. Store your leftover crackers in an airtight container in a cool, dry, and dark place for up to 1 week.

cheesy broccoli bites

MAKES ABOUT 14 BROCCOLI BITES

Broccoli is a member of the cruciferous family of veggies, or as I like to call them: super veggies. These are the veggies that I try to eat most often. Research has shown that cruciferous vegetables may help lower your risk of getting cancer. They're also rich in folate, fiber, and vitamins C, A, and K. To put it simply, they do great things for your body while making you feel full for longer. This is one of my favorite ways to eat broccoli, since when I dip them in ketchup it feels like I'm eating fried tater tots instead of these healthy baked bites. These are best enjoyed fresh rather than as leftovers. **AR**

Nonstick cooking spray, for greasing the parchment

2 cups firmly packed broccoli florets

¼ cup finely chopped yellow onion

⅓ cup nutritional yeast

⅓ cup almond flour

½ teaspoon onion powder

½ teaspoon garlic powder

¼ teaspoon table salt

Freshly ground black pepper

1 flax egg (page x)

Ketchup, for serving

Preheat the oven to 375°F. Line a baking sheet with parchment paper and lightly grease the parchment paper.

Place a medium pot of water over medium-high heat. Once the water is boiling, submerge the broccoli and cook for 3 minutes. Drain the broccoli using a colander and immediately rinse the florets under cold water. Dry them off with a paper towel.

Finely chop the broccoli using a knife or food processor (pulse until finely chopped). You should end up with about 1½ cups. Add the broccoli to a large bowl with the onion, nutritional yeast, almond flour, onion powder, garlic powder, and salt. Add pepper to taste. Stir in the flax egg and combine well. The mixture should be sticky.

Wet your hands to prevent the mixture from sticking. Take a heaping tablespoon of the mixture into your palm and form into a ball. Place the ball onto the baking sheet and press down lightly with your hand or a fork so that your broccoli bite is about ½ inch thick. Repeat with the remaining mixture until you have 14 bites.

Place your baking sheet into the oven. Bake for 10 minutes, then carefully flip each bite and bake for an additional 10 minutes. They should feel crispy to the touch and be browned on both sides. Remove from the oven and serve warm with ketchup.

crispy tofu nuggets

MAKES **12** NUGGETS

This is the recipe I make for people who think tofu is mushy and flavorless. The combination of extra-firm tofu, basic spices, and Japanese breadcrumbs creates crunchy, dippable nuggets that are bursting with savory crunch. Baking instead of frying cuts down on the calories and the mess. Don't forget to allow time for pressing the tofu; it's a key step for achieving a crispy texture. **AR**

- 1 (14 to 16-ounce) block extra-firm tofu, drained
- 1 cup gluten-free panko breadcrumbs
- ½ cup rice flour
- ¼ cup unflavored plant-based milk (any type will work)
- ½ teaspoon garlic powder
- ½ teaspoon onion powder
- ½ teaspoon cayenne pepper
- ½ teaspoon kosher salt
- 2 tablespoons tamari
- Nonstick cooking spray, for greasing the parchment paper
- Sesame Soy Mayo (page 118), for serving

Wrap the tofu in a clean and dry kitchen towel. Sandwich it between two cutting boards and then set a heavy pan, bowl, or baking dish on top of the cutting board. This will act as a weight in order to press the water out of the tofu. The weight should be heavy enough to press the tofu but not so heavy it crumbles. Let the tofu sit for at least 30 minutes. If the towel gets very saturated during this time, replace it with a fresh one.

Place the panko in a blender or food processor and pulse for 3 to 4 seconds to achieve a finer crumb.

Take out 3 small bowls and 1 medium bowl. Add the rice flour to the first small bowl. Put the plant-based milk into the second small bowl. In the third small bowl, mix together the panko, garlic powder, onion powder, cayenne pepper, and salt.

Place your pressed tofu on a cutting board with the largest surface facing up. Cut the tofu in half crosswise. Slice those halves crosswise again into sixths, which will give you 12 equal pieces.

Marinate the tofu by placing it into the medium bowl and pouring the tamari over it. Use a spoon to make sure each slice gets soaked in the tamari.

Preheat the oven to 400°F. Line a large baking sheet with parchment paper and spray it with nonstick cooking spray. Next, take one tofu slice and put it into the bowl of rice flour. Flip it over so that it's fully coated in flour. Then move the tofu to the second bowl and coat it in the milk. Lastly, place it into the panko mixture, carefully pressing the seasoned crumbs over all surfaces of the tofu to help make it stick. Place it onto the baking sheet and repeat with the remaining 11 tofu slices.

Bake the tofu for 20 minutes or until golden. Remove the baking sheet from the oven and carefully flip each slice with a spatula. Bake for an additional 20 minutes.

To serve, arrange the tofu slices onto a plate alongside a bowl of our Sesame Soy Mayo (page 118).

heart of palm calamari

SERVES **2** TO **3**

Getting creative in the kitchen is one of the things I love most about cooking. There are a lot of products out there that imitate meat, but I find that seafood can be a lot trickier to find a delicious substitute for. Enter heart of palm! This is the perfect veggie to use for calamari, since the look and texture are so similar to squid rings, especially when coated in our flavorful seasoning and fried. This is a great appetizer that will impress all of your friends. **TP**

2 (14-ounce) cans whole heart of palm

½ cup gluten-free all-purpose flour (I use King Arthur's)

¼ cup arrowroot powder

2 teaspoons seafood seasoning

½ teaspoon kosher salt

½ to 1 sheet nori (dried seaweed)

Canola oil, for frying (at least 32 ounces if using a Dutch oven)

Choice of sauce, for serving

Lemon wedges, for serving

Drain and rinse the heart of palm, then cut into 1-inch rings. You can push out the center of the larger rings for a more "calamari look." Set aside.

In a food processor, add all the dry ingredients. Use your hands to crumble the nori into smaller pieces before placing it into the processor. Pulse until everything is combined and you can still see little dark flakes of nori.

In a large mixing bowl, combine the flour mixture and the heart of palm. Toss well so every piece is coated.

In a Dutch oven or heavy-bottom pot, add the oil and bring to 350°F. Working in batches, fry the heart of palm until golden brown, about 2 to 3 minutes. Serve with Garlicky Lemon Aioli (page 114), marinara, or our Tartar Sauce (page 114). Serve with lemon wedges, if desired.

blistered shishito peppers

SERVES 4

This small plate is a real crowd-pleaser that sounds and looks impressive but is super easy to make. Shishito peppers are very mild, but about one in ten can be spicy, making this low-calorie and vitamin-rich veggie an exciting surprise! **AR**

8 ounces shishito peppers, about 16 peppers

2 teaspoons avocado oil

2 teaspoons flaky sea salt, plus additional as needed

Finely grated zest of ½ lemon

Rinse the peppers and pat them dry. Place in a large mixing bowl. Add the oil and toss to coat.

Heat a large skillet over medium heat. The skillet is ready when a drop of water sizzles and evaporates upon contact with the surface.

Carefully add the peppers to the skillet, making sure each one is in contact with the skillet. Cook for about 2 minutes before stirring them around. Cook for an additional 3 to 4 minutes. The peppers should be charred and wilted. Remove from heat and add the salt and lemon zest. Add more salt to taste. Transfer the peppers to a bowl and serve immediately, with an additional empty bowl to discard the stems.

CHAPTER

3

soup, there it is!

and salad

shredded brussels sprouts salad

SERVES 4

While you might be used to seeing Brussels sprouts boiled, roasted, or fried, they make the perfect salad base when they are raw and finely shredded. They're crunchy, take on the flavor of any dressing, and they're one of the most protein-rich veggies out there. I still throw in almonds and hemp hearts for additional protein and texture, and the dates add the perfect amount of sweetness. **AR**

1 pound Brussels sprouts

1 apple (I like Honeycrisp), cored and chopped into small cubes

½ cup slivered almonds

½ cup pitted Deglet Noor dates, coarsely chopped

¼ cup hemp hearts

Orange Vinaigrette (page 113)

Rinse the Brussels sprouts. Trim the bottoms (the stems can be hard and dry) and remove the outer leaves. Slice them finely, either using a very sharp knife or the slicing blade on a food processor. Add the shredded sprouts to a large salad bowl along with the apple, almonds, dates, and hemp hearts.

Serve with a drizzle of our Orange Vinaigrette. Add just enough to coat everything and toss well before serving.

avocado salad

SERVES 2 TO 3

This is a super-simple and colorful salad that is rich with vitamins and omega-3 fatty acids. A perfect side for Taco Tuesday or when you want a quick and easy snack. **TP**

6 ripe avocados

2 cups halved cherry tomatoes

½ cup diced yellow onion

Juice of 1 lime

2 tablespoons extra-virgin olive oil

Kosher salt and freshly ground black pepper

Microgreens, optional

Remove the pits from the avocados and dice into bite-size pieces, similar in size to the sliced tomatoes.

Add the avocados, tomatoes, onion, and lime juice to a medium mixing bowl. Stir gently to combine. Season to taste with salt and pepper. Let the salad sit in the refrigerator for at least 10 minutes before serving. Remove from the fridge, garnish with microgreens, and serve.

peach kale salad

SERVES 4

This is a nutrient bomb of a salad. We've put all our favorite things in here. The homemade candied pecans are so good that they might not make it into the salad, and that's OK too. **AR**

salad

¼ cup dry quinoa, rinsed using a fine-mesh colander

½ cup room-temperature water

2 cups coarsely chopped stemmed kale

Dash of fresh lemon juice

Pinch of flaky sea salt

2 peaches, pitted and sliced

candied pecans

2 tablespoons maple syrup

1 tablespoon room-temperature water

¼ teaspoon pure vanilla extract

½ teaspoon ground cinnamon

Pinch of kosher salt

1 cup raw pecan halves

Maple Tahini Dressing (page 112)

For the salad, add the quinoa and water to a medium saucepan. Bring to a boil over medium-high heat. Cover the saucepan and decrease the heat to low. Simmer for 10 to 15 minutes, or until the water is absorbed and the quinoa is tender. Remove from the heat and let rest, covered, for 5 minutes. Fluff the quinoa with a fork and set aside.

For the candied pecans, whisk together the maple syrup, water, vanilla, cinnamon, and salt in a small bowl.

Place a piece of parchment paper on a small baking sheet.

Heat up a medium skillet over medium-high heat. Add the pecans and toast them for 3 minutes, stirring occasionally. Pour the maple syrup mixture over the pecans, stirring the nuts as you pour. Continuously stir until the pecans are completely coated and the liquid has evaporated. Remove from the heat.

Spread the pecans on the lined baking sheet so that they are not touching each other. Allow to cool while preparing the rest of the salad.

Place the kale in a large salad bowl. Add a dash of fresh lemon juice and a pinch of sea salt. Massage the kale with your hands, crunching the leaves between your fingers, until they just start to wilt.

Add the quinoa, peaches, and half of the candied pecans. (Store the rest of the pecans in an airtight container for next time or a snack!)

Serve topped with Maple Tahini Dressing, using as much or as little as desired. Toss well before serving.

kale caesar

SERVES 3 TO 4

Let's jazz up this salad and use kale! Kale is such a great vehicle for this homemade dressing and is full of antioxidants, vitamins, and minerals. In fact, kale is so rich in nutrients, especially calcium, that it's even known as the king of the super-greens. Massaging the kale really makes a difference, and it is totally worth the extra effort; you will not be disappointed. **TP**

dressing
(makes 1 cup)

¾ cup raw cashews

3½ cups plus 2 tablespoons water, divided

3 cloves garlic

Freshly squeezed juice of 1 lemon

1 tablespoon Dijon mustard

1 tablespoon capers

½ teaspoon kosher salt

¼ teaspoon freshly ground black pepper

salad

7 cups chopped kale

1 tablespoon olive oil

2 cups sliced cherry or grape tomatoes, for garnish

4 tablespoons pumpkin seeds, for garnish

Vegan croutons, for garnish

For the dressing, place the cashews and 3 cups of water in a medium saucepan and boil on high for 2 minutes; turn down to medium and cover with a lid to boil for an additional 28 minutes, or until the cashews are tender. Using a strainer, drain the cashews of any remaining water and rinse with cold water. Then combine the cashews, garlic, lemon juice, capers, salt, pepper, and the remaining ½ cup and 2 tablespoons of water in a high-speed blender until smooth. Set aside.

Make the salad in a large mixing bowl by combining the kale and olive oil. Using your hands, massage the oil into the kale until the kale becomes softer, about 1 to 2 minutes. Add the tomatoes.

Pour in the dressing and mix until the tomatoes and kale are completely covered.

Transfer the salad to individual bowls or a large serving dish and top with pumpkin seeds and vegan croutons.

note

To make the dressing thinner, add more water, 1 tablespoon at a time. You can use as much or as little dressing as you'd like.

Thai salad

SERVES 4 TO 6

This salad has it all! It's hearty and full of beautiful ingredients and textures. This is the perfect salad to bring to a party or outdoor barbecue. Most salads don't make great leftovers, especially after being dressed, but because this salad has a noodle base, it still tastes amazing after a couple of days soaking in the sauce in the fridge. **TP**

1 (6 to 8-ounce pack) rice noodles

1 tablespoon peanut oil

1 cup shredded carrots

½ cup diced cucumber

4 cups shredded purple cabbage

1 red bell pepper, seeded and thinly sliced

Peanut Dressing (page 116)

½ cup chopped fresh cilantro, for garnish

½ cup crushed unsalted peanuts, for garnish

3 scallions, finely chopped, green and white parts, for garnish

2 limes, quartered, for garnish

Cook the rice noodles per the package instructions. Drain and toss with peanut oil and set aside.

In a large bowl or serving platter, combine the carrots, cucumbers, cabbage, red bell pepper, and rice noodles. Add enough Peanut Dressing to coat everything and toss well. Garnish with the cilantro, peanuts, scallions, and limes.

notes

If you have a peanut allergy, substitute the peanut butter in the dressing with almond butter and the peanuts with sliced almonds.

Store leftovers in a sealed container in the fridge for up to 3 days.

tomato-basil with grilled cheese croutons

SERVES 6 TO 8

Tomato soup has always been one of my favorites. Growing up, my mom used to make this all the time. As soon as the seasons would change, which, to be honest, isn't much in Florida, I knew it was time for this warm and comforting soup. I love to use coconut milk in this recipe because it adds a rich creaminess that I craved as a kid. **TP**

soup

3 tablespoons vegan butter

1 medium yellow onion, diced

3 cloves garlic, minced

7 medium on-the-vine tomatoes, quartered

3 to 4 tablespoons cane sugar

1 teaspoon chopped fresh oregano

10 large fresh basil leaves, plus extra for serving

2 cups vegetable broth

Kosher salt and freshly ground black pepper

1 cup canned coconut milk

croutons

4 slices vegan cheese

8 slices vegan bread

Vegan butter, for spreading

½ cup roughly chopped basil, for garnish

To make the soup, place the butter in a large pot or Dutch oven over medium heat. When it is melted, add the onion and garlic and cook for 3 to 4 minutes, until the onion is translucent. Next, add the tomatoes, and add the sugar to taste. Stir to combine with the onions and garlic. Allow the tomatoes to cook down for about 7 to 10 minutes. They should lose most of their shape.

Add the oregano and basil and stir to combine. Pour in the vegetable broth and turn the heat up to a boil for 1 minute then down to a simmer. Season with salt and pepper to taste. Using an immersion blender, pulse together the soup mixture until creamy with no visible chunks. You can also work carefully in batches using a blender. Return all the blended soup to the pot. Stir in the coconut milk and simmer for an additional 10 to 15 minutes.

While the soup is simmering, make the grilled cheese croutons. Assemble the sandwiches with 1 slice of cheese and two pieces of bread, spreading the butter on the tops and bottoms of the sandwiches.

In a skillet over medium-high heat, cook the sandwiches 2 to 3 minutes on each side.

Cut into small square pieces and serve on top of the soup with a few pieces of basil.

lemony lentil soup

SERVES 4 TO 6

Lentils are a great source of protein, and this soup can prove it. Hearty and full of bright, fresh lemony flavor, I could eat this year-round. **TP**

4 tablespoons vegan butter

2 large carrots, peeled and diced

1 medium yellow onion, diced

3 cloves garlic, minced

2 teaspoons ground cumin

½ teaspoon turmeric

2 teaspoons nutritional yeast

1 cup uncooked green lentils

6 cups vegetable broth

Juice of 2 lemons

Finely grated zest of 1 lemon

Kosher salt and freshly ground black pepper

Place the vegan butter in a Dutch oven or heavy-bottom pot over medium heat. Next, add the carrots and onion and sauté for 4 to 5 minutes. Add the garlic and sauté for an additional 1 to 2 minutes.

Next, sprinkle in the ground cumin, turmeric, and nutritional yeast. Stir well and cook for 1 to 2 minutes.

Pour in the dry lentils and allow them to toast for 1 minute or so, stirring frequently.

Now, pour in the vegetable broth, lemon juice, and lemon zest. Bring to a boil and then decrease to a simmer to allow the lentils to cook, about 20 minutes.

Once the lentils are tender, add salt and pepper to taste.

Using an immersion blender, blend until the soup is thicker in texture and most lentil shapes have disappeared. If you do not have an immersion blender, you can use a normal high-speed blender, working in batches. Warm the soup over low heat and serve.

spicy Thai butternut squash soup

SERVES 6

Thai red curry paste puts a fun and spicy twist on traditional butternut squash soup. I know it doesn't get very cold in Los Angeles, but any time the sun isn't out, I love making this bright and warming recipe. Avocado slices on top give it Cali vibes. **AR**

2 tablespoons coconut oil

1 large yellow onion, peeled and coarsely chopped

3 cloves garlic, chopped

1 tablespoon peeled, finely chopped ginger

2 tablespoons Thai red curry paste

1 (2-pound) butternut squash, peeled, seeded, cut into large ¾-inch dice

3 cups vegetable broth

1 (15-ounce) canned coconut milk, divided

Juice of 1 lime, plus additional for serving

Kosher salt and freshly ground black pepper

Finely sliced avocado and chopped fresh cilantro, for garnish

Heat the coconut oil in a large pot over medium heat. Add the onion and sauté for 5 minutes. Add the garlic and sauté for an additional 2 minutes, stirring frequently. Add the ginger and curry paste and stir to combine. Cook for 3 minutes.

Add the squash and carefully pour in the vegetable broth. Stir. Bring to a boil, cover, and decrease the heat to medium-low. Cook for about 20 minutes, or until the squash is tender. Remove from the heat.

Add half of the coconut milk and then add the lime juice to the soup.

Now to blend the soup, you can use an immersion blender or a normal blender. If using an immersion blender, puree the soup directly in the pot until smooth. Add salt and pepper to taste. Transfer the soup to individual bowls for serving.

If you do not have an immersion blender, you can use a normal high-speed blender, working in batches. If needed, return the blended soup to the pot and warm it up over medium heat to your desired temperature. Add salt and pepper to taste. Transfer the soup to individual bowls.

For serving, I like to top each bowl of soup with a dash of fresh lime juice, a spoonful of coconut milk, avocado slices, and fresh cilantro. Store leftover soup in a sealed container in the fridge for up to 4 days or in the freezer for up to 1 month.

cream of mushroom soup

SERVES 4 TO 6

I absolutely love mushrooms. I could put them on or in just about everything. A whole pot dedicated to this tasty fungus? Sign me up! This soup is creamy, rich, and packed with flavor. **TP**

4 tablespoons vegan butter

8 ounces baby Bella mushrooms, roughly chopped

8 ounces white mushrooms, roughly chopped

½ medium yellow onion, diced

3 cloves garlic, minced

1 teaspoon fresh thyme

2 tablespoons cornstarch

3 cups vegetable broth

1 (13.5-ounce) canned coconut milk

1 teaspoon vegan Worcestershire sauce

1 teaspoon kosher salt

Freshly ground black pepper

Place the butter in a Dutch oven or heavy-bottom pot over medium heat to melt. Next, add the mushrooms and onions. Sauté for 5 to 7 minutes, stirring occasionally, until soft. Add the garlic and thyme and sauté for an additional 1 to 2 minutes.

Sprinkle in the cornstarch to coat all the veggies and cook for 1 to 2 minutes.

Add the vegetable broth, coconut milk, Worcestershire sauce, and salt. Bring to a boil, then turn down to a simmer.

Using an immersion blender, blend until smooth and most of the mushroom pieces are broken down. If you do not have an immersion blender, you can use a normal high-speed blender, working in batches. Add in the pepper to taste and let the soup simmer for 10 to 15 minutes before serving.

get * on * our

g**d sides

sesame noodles

SERVES 2

OK, y'all, these noodles are everything. I love making these as a side or sometimes as a main. This recipe is so easy, it's insane: boil the noodles, mix the sauce ingredients together with some noodle water, and there you have it. A dish so good your guests won't believe it took 10 minutes to make. **TP**

1 (10-ounce) package brown rice udon noodles

2 tablespoons tahini or sesame paste

3 tablespoons tamari

1 teaspoon chili oil or paste

1 teaspoon toasted sesame oil

½ teaspoon rice vinegar

1 tablespoon dark-brown sugar

Chopped scallions and crushed peanuts, for garnish

Cook the udon noodles per the directions on the package, reserve ¼ of the noodle water, and then drain the noodles and set aside. You can toss the noodles with a little bit of extra sesame oil while you're making the sauce so that the noodles don't stick together.

To make the sauce, whisk together the tahini paste, tamari, chili oil, sesame oil, rice vinegar, sugar, and reserved noodle water in a bowl. Once the sauce is mixed well, place the noodles in a large bowl and pour the sauce on top. Toss the noodles with the sauce.

Served with chopped scallions and chopped peanuts on top.

creamed corn

SERVES 4 TO 6

I REALLY LOVE CORN! No, seriously. Grilled, roasted, sautéed—you name it, I'll take it. The fresh corn really makes a difference in this dish, and I promise it's not difficult, but please be careful when cutting it! **TP**

8 fresh corn cobs

3 tablespoons vegan butter

1 medium yellow onion, diced

3 cloves garlic, minced

1 teaspoon freshly chopped rosemary

2 tablespoons cornstarch

1 cup canned coconut milk

¼ cup unsweetened plant-based milk (I use almond or soy milk)

Kosher salt and freshly ground black pepper

To remove the corn kernels from the cobs, in a large bowl, hold the cob upright and, using a sharp knife, gently cut the kernels off going downward.

In a large skillet over medium heat, add the corn, butter, and onion and sauté for 3 to 5 minutes, until the onions are translucent. Add the garlic and rosemary and sauté for an additional minute. Sprinkle in the cornstarch and let cook for 1 minute, frequently stirring.

Pour in the two milks, stirring thoroughly. Turn the heat down to a simmer for 10 minutes and allow to thicken. Season with salt and pepper to taste.

Sichuan green beans

SERVES 4

Green beans are low in calories but rich in nutrients, making them a great veggie to add to your diet. They are rich in numerous vitamins, including vitamin K, which studies have linked to healthy bones. However, they can be pretty boring if not cooked or seasoned properly, and I avoided them until my mom made me this recipe. The beans are tender but not soggy, and the flavors are bold but not overpowering. I recommend having some rice on the side to soak up the yummy sauce. **AR**

1 tablespoon toasted sesame oil

¼ cup tamari

1½ tablespoons hoisin sauce

2 tablespoons granulated sugar

3 cloves garlic, minced

½ tablespoon peanut oil

16 ounces haricot verts, rinsed and ends trimmed

Toasted sesame seeds, for garnish

Make a sauce by whisking together the sesame oil, tamari, hoisin sauce, sugar, and garlic. Set aside.

Heat the peanut oil in a skillet over high heat. Add the haricot verts and sauté for 1 to 2 minutes, tossing frequently. Pour the sauce over the haricot verts and decrease the heat to low. Simmer for 2 minutes, or until the beans are tender.

Transfer to a serving dish and garnish with toasted sesame seeds.

roasted root veg

SERVES 3 TO 4

This side dish is super simple to assemble and will have your guests wondering how you did it! Packed full of flavor, this partnership of root vegetables will elevate any main dish. **TP**

4 large carrots, washed and peeled

3 medium parsnips, washed and peeled

4 sprigs fresh rosemary

¼ cup vegetable broth

1 teaspoon Dijon mustard

1 tablespoon maple syrup

4 tablespoons melted vegan butter

Preheat the oven to 425°F.

Cut the carrots and parsnips lengthwise so that you get about 4 slices per vegetable.

In a large 9 by 13-inch rectangle baking dish, mix the rosemary, broth, mustard, maple syrup, and melted butter together. Add the sliced vegetables. Using your hands or tongs, toss a few times so all the vegetables are coated.

Bake for 50 to 55 minutes or until fork tender. Serve with your favorite main.

mac and cheese without all the crap

SERVES 8 TO 10

When my Football Ferns teammate Daisy Cleverley told me she had created a plant-based cheese sauce without using any vegan cheese products, I literally raced to the kitchen to try it for myself. I was immediately hooked and begged her to let me publish my version in a cookbook one day. Luckily, she said yes, and here we are! This is not like the powdered cheese sauce from the boxed mac and cheese that I grew up on, and it's not your Southern-baked classic either. It's a wonderfully different version that is thick, creamy, and rich in umami. I eat this mac and cheese at least once a week, and on any given day you can also find me dipping my tortilla chips in the sauce. This can be served as a side or a main dish. **AR**

1 sweet potato, peeled and cut into 1-inch cubes

½ medium yellow onion, roughly chopped

16 ounces elbow macaroni or any short pasta noodle (rotini is my personal favorite)

½ cup raw cashews

⅓ cup nutritional yeast

½ cup canned coconut milk

Freshly squeezed juice of 1 lemon

2 teaspoons garlic powder

2 teaspoons kosher salt, plus additional as needed

Bring a large pot of water to a boil. There should be enough water in the pot to cover the sweet potato by at least 1 inch. Carefully add the sweet potato and onion. Decrease the heat to medium-high and cook the vegetables until the sweet potato can be pierced with a fork, about 10 to 12 minutes. Transfer the sweet potato and onion to a colander and drain.

While the sweet potato and onion are cooking, you can boil your pasta. Fill a large pot with water and bring to a boil. Add the pasta and cook according to the manufacturer's directions. Reserve ½ cup of the pasta water before transferring the pasta to a colander and draining it. Rinse the drained pasta under cold running water and set aside.

Place the sweet potato, onion, cashews, nutritional yeast, coconut milk, lemon juice, garlic powder, and kosher salt into a blender. Add ¼ cup of the pasta water. Blend until smooth. Add more water as needed to reach your desired sauce consistency. The sauce is usually still warm from the cooked veggies, but if you want it hotter, you can reheat it in a medium saucepan over medium heat before serving.

Add the cooked pasta to a large serving bowl and spoon a desired amount of sauce on top. I like a lot of sauce per noodle! Mix well to coat the noodles in the sauce. Add additional salt to taste. Store leftovers in a sealed container in the fridge for up to 3 days. Reheat in a saucepan on low heat or in the microwave, checking the temperature every 15 seconds.

roasted garlic dill potatoes

SERVES 4 TO 6

While playing and living in Russia, I fell in love with dill; it's everywhere in the cuisine! The dill in this recipe really makes these beautiful carbs shine. This side pairs well with almost anything and is so easy to make. **TP**

1 pound small red potatoes, washed and cut in half

6 tablespoons melted vegan butter

¾ cup vegetable broth

7 cloves garlic, minced

Freshly squeezed juice of 1 lemon

3 tablespoons freshly chopped dill, plus more for garnish

1 teaspoon kosher salt

Preheat the oven to 425°F.

In a large 9 by 13-inch rectangle baking dish, add all the ingredients. Toss using your hands or a large spoon to make sure all the potatoes are coated well.

Bake for 50 to 55 minutes or until the potatoes are fork tender. Remove from the oven and serve with more chopped dill and additional lemon juice squeezed over the top, if you like.

the main

characters

chickpea curry wrap

SERVES 2 TO 3

This wrap is full of flavor and packed with protein. Because the chickpeas are mashed, even our "chickpea-wary" friends love this recipe. Perfect for any lunch, picnic, or quick bite. **TP**

2 (15-ounce) cans chickpeas, rinsed and drained

1 cup vegan mayonnaise

1 tablespoon Dijon mustard

1 tablespoon curry powder

½ medium red onion, diced

2 green onion stalks, chopped

1 cup sliced grape or cherry tomatoes

½ cup chopped walnuts

Kosher salt and freshly ground black pepper

Tortillas or wrap of choice

Place the chickpeas in a large mixing bowl and smash with the back of a fork or masher. Smash them until most of the chickpeas no longer have their original shape.

Mix in the mayonnaise, Dijon mustard, and curry powder. Combine well. Next, add the red onion, green onions, tomatoes, and walnuts, stirring well to make sure everything is coated.

Season with salt and pepper to taste. Refrigerate for 20 minutes before serving.

Serve in your favorite tortilla or wrap.

lentil sloppy joes

SERVES 4 TO 6

We love lentils for being a great source of protein, but I also love them for their versatility. This spin on a classic is so hearty and nostalgic while still giving you that Sloppy Joe texture and taste. **TP**

1 cup uncooked green lentils, rinsed

2 tablespoons olive oil

1 small yellow onion, diced

1 green bell pepper, seeded and diced

3 cloves garlic, minced

1 tablespoon chili powder

1 teaspoon kosher salt

1 (8-ounce) can tomato sauce

½ cup vegan barbecue sauce

1 tablespoon Dijon mustard

1 tablespoon vegan and gluten-free Worcestershire sauce or tamari

2 teaspoons liquid smoke

1 teaspoon apple cider vinegar

2 tablespoons dark-brown sugar

Vegan butter, for spreading

Hamburger buns of choice

Fill a large pot halfway with water. Bring to a boil and add the lentils. Boil for 2 minutes, then cover with a lid and decrease the heat to simmer for 20 minutes. When the lentils are done, strain and set aside.

In a skillet over medium heat, add the olive oil, onion, and green bell pepper. Sauté for 5 to 6 minutes, until the onions are translucent. Add the garlic and sauté for an additional 1 to 2 minutes.

Sprinkle in the chili powder and salt, and cook for 1 minute. Add the tomato sauce, barbecue sauce, Dijon mustard, Worcestershire sauce, liquid smoke, and apple cider vinegar. Stir well. Pour in ½ cup water and mix thoroughly to combine. Sprinkle in the sugar and stir, then add the cooked lentils.

Turn down to a simmer and cook for 10 to 15 minutes, stirring occasionally. Butter each side of the buns and toast lightly in the oven for 2 to 3 minutes. Assemble the sloppy joes and enjoy!

tlt

SERVES **5**

BLTs will forever remind me of my grandmother. She would always make them for me when I was younger, and I knew when writing this book that I had to recreate those same flavors and summer memories. Utilizing tofu as bacon is a great way to ensure protein and nutrients while still having that classic BLT flavor. **TP**

1 (16-ounce) block extra-firm tofu

⅓ cup tamari

3 tablespoons maple syrup

2 tablespoons liquid smoke

2 tablespoons tomato paste

1 teaspoon vegan Worcestershire sauce

1 teaspoon smoked paprika

Nonstick cooking spray, for greasing the baking sheet

10 slices of your favorite bread

Garlicky Lemon Aioli (page 114)

Butter lettuce

2 to 3 large tomatoes, sliced

Preheat the oven to 375°F.

Rinse and drain the tofu, then pat dry with a tea towel or paper towel. Try to gently squeeze out any remaining liquid.

Slice the tofu into very thin layers; you should be able to get 15 to 16 ⅛-inch slices.

In a large mixing bowl, whisk together the tamari, maple syrup, liquid smoke, tomato paste, Worcestershire sauce, and paprika. Gently place the tofu into the bowl so that all slices are covered in liquid. Marinate in the refrigerator for at least 1 hour.

Spray a large baking sheet with nonstick spray. Lay out the tofu slices so they are evenly spaced and bake for 20 minutes. Flip and brush with some of the remaining marinade and bake for an additional 15 to 20 minutes.

Assemble a sandwich by lightly toasting 2 slices of bread then spreading the Garlicky Lemon Aioli on both sides. Lay 3 slices of tofu on 1 slice of bread, followed by lettuce and tomato and then the other slice of bread. Repeat with the remaining ingredients to finish the sandwiches.

coconut cauliflower tacos

SERVES 2 TO 4

Crunchy, sweet, spicy, and zesty. We have taken veggie tacos to the next level with this baked coconut-coated cauliflower. Make these tacos for your next Taco Tuesday, and don't forget the Spicy Grapefruit Margaritas (page 129)! **TP**

1 medium head cauliflower

¾ cup canned coconut milk

Finely grated zest and juice of 1 lime

¾ teaspoon kosher salt, divided

1 cup gluten-free panko breadcrumbs

½ cup cornmeal

½ cup shredded coconut

1 teaspoon garlic powder

1 teaspoon onion powder

½ teaspoon chili powder

Sweet and Spicy Mayo (page 118)

Tortillas and taco toppings, for serving

Preheat the oven to 400°F.

Slice the cauliflower into bite-size pieces.

In a medium bowl, combine the coconut milk, lime zest and juice, and ¼ teaspoon of the salt. In another medium bowl, mix the breadcrumbs, cornmeal, shredded coconut, garlic powder, onion powder, chili powder, and the remaining ½ teaspoon of salt.

Line a baking sheet with parchment paper. Set the bowls next to each other and dip the cauliflower pieces into the wet batter, then dry-mix to coat and place onto the lined baking sheet. Repeat this step until all the cauliflower is battered.

Bake for 20 minutes, flipping the cauliflower after 10 minutes.

Serve and enjoy with the Sweet and Spicy Mayo and your favorite tortillas and toppings.

note

Sweetened coconut flakes work best for this, such as Baker's Angel Flake Coconut.

mushroom tofu lettuce wraps

SERVES 8

The tofu may provide the protein, but for me, the mushrooms are the star of this show. I'm always amazed at how meaty mushrooms can be, and when they are coated with ginger marinade and wrapped in a crispy lettuce leaf, you've got yourself a real dinner party hit. And trust me, the messiness is part of the fun! Serve with a side of your favorite rice if you're fueling up for a workout. **AR**

½ tablespoon peeled and grated fresh ginger

1 clove garlic, minced

2 tablespoons tamari

1½ tablespoons hoisin sauce

1 tablespoon freshly squeezed lime juice

2 tablespoons peanut oil

1 (14 to 16-ounce) block extra-firm tofu, drained

½ cup finely chopped carrot

8 ounces cremini mushrooms, finely chopped

1 (8-ounce) can sliced water chestnuts, drained and finely chopped

2 scallions, finely chopped, plus additional for topping

8 large leaves butter lettuce, for serving

Hoisin Peanut Sauce (page 117), for garnish

Cooked rice, for serving, optional

In a small bowl, whisk together the ginger, garlic, tamari, hoisin sauce, and lime juice. Set aside.

Heat the peanut oil in a large skillet over medium-high heat. Using your hands, crumble up the tofu into the skillet, breaking it into even smaller pieces with a spatula (think Tofu Scramble texture). Add the carrot and cook for 5 minutes. Add the mushrooms and cook for 3 minutes, until the mixture is starting to brown and the liquid has mostly evaporated. Add the water chestnuts and scallions and cook for 1 minute. Pour in the ginger sauce and stir to combine. Remove from the heat.

Serve with the lettuce leaves and our Hoisin Peanut Sauce. To make a lettuce wrap, take a leaf in your palm and fill it with a scoop of the filling. Add a dollop of sauce. Wrap up and enjoy. Serve with a side of rice, if desired.

mushroom risotto

SERVES 4 TO 6

Want an elevated dish? Look no further! This risotto is perfect for date night or any special occasion. I think most people are intimidated by the thought of making risotto, and I'm here to tell you that it's easier than you think. With some patience and love, you'll be a risotto master in no time. **TP**

1 tablespoon vegan butter

2 tablespoons olive oil

½ medium yellow onion, diced

1 (8-ounce) package baby Bella mushrooms, roughly chopped

3 cloves garlic, minced

2 cups Arborio rice

1 cup dry vegan white wine

6 cups vegetable broth

¼ to ½ cup Cashew Cream (page viii)

½ cup frozen peas

Finely grated zest and juice of 1 lemon, plus additional juice, for serving

Kosher salt and freshly ground black pepper

Place the butter and olive oil in a large skillet over medium heat. Add the onion and mushrooms. Sauté for 5 to 7 minutes, until the onions are translucent. Add the garlic and sauté for an additional 2 minutes.

Add the Arborio rice and stir thoroughly. Toast the rice for 1 to 2 minutes. Pour in the white wine and cook until fully absorbed, stirring constantly. Next, pour in 1 cup of the vegetable broth and stir constantly until the liquid is absorbed by the rice. Repeat this step with the remaining 5 cups of vegetable broth, adding 1 cup at a time until the liquid has evaporated.

Once all the broth is absorbed and the rice is tender, turn down the heat to low and stir in the Cashew Cream, peas, and lemon zest and juice. Stir to incorporate well. Season with salt and pepper to taste. Serve with additional freshly squeezed lemon juice over the top, if you like.

creamy black bean and corn enchiladas

MAKES 8 ENCHILADAS

This is my favorite meal to eat the night before a game, especially because it makes so many leftovers and I can enjoy them for a few days after the game too! These enchiladas are packed with protein and flavor but still feel like comfort food. I've served this to my parents, and they had no clue that it was vegan. If you can't find red enchilada sauce, you can use jarred red salsa instead. If using vegan shredded cheese for the topping, I highly recommend using one that you know melts. Not all vegan cheeses do! **AR**

1 cup jarred red salsa (mild, medium, or hot, depending on your preference)

6 to 8 ounces firm tofu

¼ cup nutritional yeast

Room-temperature water, as needed

2 tablespoons avocado oil

½ large red onion, finely chopped

3 cloves garlic, minced

1 large red or yellow bell pepper, seeded and cut into medium (½-inch) dice

3 cups firmly packed spinach

Table salt

1 (15-ounce) can black beans, rinsed and drained

1 (8.25-ounce) can whole kernel corn, drained

8 (8-inch) flour tortillas

2 cups red enchilada sauce (mild or medium, depending on preference), divided

2 cups shredded vegan cheese, for garnish

Lime wedges, guacamole, salsa, and fresh cilantro, for serving

Continued

Preheat the oven to 350°F.

In a blender, add the salsa, tofu, and nutritional yeast. Blend on low for 1 minute, or until smooth, scraping down the sides of the blender as needed. If necessary to help the blending process, add water 1 tablespoon at a time. Set aside.

Heat the oil in a large skillet over medium-high heat. Add the onion and sauté for 2 minutes, until slightly softened and turning translucent. Add the garlic and sauté for 1 minute more. Add the bell pepper and spinach and stir until the leaves are wilted, about 3 minutes.

Decrease the heat to low. Add the salsa mixture and salt to taste. Mix well. Stir in the black beans and corn. Remove from the heat.

Add ½ cup enchilada sauce to the bottom of a 9 by 13-inch casserole dish. Take a tortilla in your hand and spoon approximately ¼ cup of filling into the tortilla. Roll it up and place it, seam side down, into the casserole dish. Repeat with the remaining filling and tortillas. Pour the remaining 1½ cups of enchilada sauce over the rolled-up tortillas. Sprinkle the cheese over the top, if using.

Bake for 20 minutes, or until the tortillas are golden brown and slightly crispy on the outside.

Serve with lime wedges, guacamole, salsa, and fresh cilantro. Store leftovers in a sealed container in the fridge for up to 3 days. Reheat in the microwave, checking the temperature every 30 seconds, or in the oven for 20 minutes at 350°F. Unless I'm in a rush, I prefer the oven method because it gets the tortillas crispy again.

cauliflower fried rice

SERVES 4

Getting people who don't like veggies to eat veggies is one of my joys in life, because we really do need our veggies, especially as athletes who put an enormous amount of strain on our bodies. But forcing down food you don't like doesn't have to be the answer. There are so many awesome ways to prepare vegetables that make eating them enjoyable. Sometimes it's just about being creative. This recipe substitutes riced cauliflower for rice, which gets you eating an entire bowl of cauliflower without even realizing it. The addition of tofu instead of egg makes sure you still get your protein. **AR**

2 tablespoons peanut oil, divided

6 to 8 ounces firm tofu, drained

1 medium head cauliflower, rinsed

2 cloves garlic, minced

1 large carrot, peeled and chopped into medium (½-inch) dice

½ small white onion, finely chopped

1 cup frozen green peas

¼ cup tamari

3 green onion stalks, green parts only, finely chopped

Table salt and freshly ground black pepper

Heat 1 tablespoon of peanut oil in a small skillet over medium-high heat.

Using your hands, crumble the tofu into the skillet. Cook the tofu, stirring frequently, for 3 to 4 minutes, until it has some color and the water from the tofu has cooked off. Remove from the heat and set aside.

Remove any leaves from the cauliflower and chop off the stem. Separate the head into medium-size florets using your hands or a knife. Working in batches, place a few florets in a food processor at a time and pulse for a few seconds, until the texture is like rice. Be careful not to overprocess the cauliflower or you will have mushy rice.

Heat the remaining 1 tablespoon of peanut oil in a large sauté pan or wok over high heat. Add the garlic, carrots, and white onion and cook for 1 minute. Add the cauliflower and cook until softened, stirring frequently, about 5 to 6 minutes. Mix in the peas and scrambled tofu. Pour over the tamari and stir to combine. Add the green onions and season with salt and pepper to taste.

To serve, I like to pack the rice into a small round bowl and flip it over onto a plate.

butter chickpeas and potatoes

SERVES 4 TO 6

Yum, yum, yum! That's all I can say about this recipe. The spices really warm up this dish, and the coconut cream gives it such richness. I love to eat this the night before a game, paired with rice. It gives me everything I need: carbs, protein, and a full belly. **TP**

4 tablespoons vegan butter

1 medium yellow onion, finely diced

5 cloves garlic, minced

1 tablespoon peeled and minced fresh ginger

1½ teaspoons garam masala

1 teaspoon ground cumin

1 teaspoon chili powder

1 teaspoon coriander

½ teaspoon kosher salt

1 (14.5-ounce) can crushed tomatoes, with juices

1 cup Thai coconut cream

1 tablespoon light-brown sugar

1 large russet potato, peeled, washed, and cubed (about the same size as the chickpeas)

2 (15-ounce) cans chickpeas, drained and rinsed

Fresh cilantro, for garnish

Cooked rice, for serving

Place the butter and onion in a Dutch oven or heavy-bottom pot over medium heat. Sauté for 3 to 4 minutes. Add the garlic and ginger and sauté for an additional 1 to 2 minutes.

Sprinkle in all the spices and cook for 1 minute, stirring frequently so that the spices have a chance to cook. Pour in the tomatoes. Stir to incorporate everything and lower the heat to a simmer.

Using an immersion blender, blend until the liquid becomes more like a creamy soup. If you do not have an immersion blender, carefully scoop the tomato contents into a blender. Pulse until smooth and pour back into the pot. Then add the coconut cream, sugar, potatoes, and chickpeas. Mix well and bring to a boil for 1 minute. Then turn down to a simmer for 30 minutes, or until the potatoes are tender.

Garnish with fresh cilantro. Serve over rice or eat it alone.

heart of palm cakes

SERVES 3 TO 4

These are a crowd-pleaser! When I first became vegan, I really missed seafood. Heart of palm is a wonderful replacement and is so versatile. This is a dish I make for people who are new to vegan food or who are looking for familiarity. I love to see the looks on people's faces when they realize just how tasty it is. These cakes go well with Creamed Corn (page 57) served on the side, or they also make lovely appetizers as well. To make this dish as an appetizer, simply make the cakes smaller and decrease the frying time by 1 minute. You should get about 12 to 16 cakes. **TP**

1 tablespoon avocado oil, plus more for frying

½ medium yellow onion, finely diced

½ red bell pepper, seeded and finely diced

1 stalk celery, finely diced

2 cloves garlic, minced

1 (14-ounce) can hearts of palm

1 (14-ounce) can artichoke hearts

1 (15-ounce) can chickpeas

3 teaspoons seafood seasoning

1 teaspoon kosher salt

½ cup vegan mayo

1¼ cups gluten-free panko breadcrumbs, divided

Lemon wedges and Tartar Sauce (page 114), for serving

In a skillet over medium heat, add the 1 tablespoon of avocado oil, the onion, bell pepper, and celery. Sauté for 4 to 5 minutes, until the diced onions are translucent. Add the garlic and sauté for an additional 2 minutes, then remove from the heat and transfer to a bowl. Carefully wipe the pan clean.

While the veggies are cooling, drain the hearts of palm and artichoke hearts. (You might need to give the artichokes a good squeeze to remove any excess water.) Then chop both into very small pieces, slightly bigger than the diced veggies, and set aside. Drain and rinse the chickpeas, then mash them with a potato masher or the back of a fork until they no longer have their round shape and set aside.

In a large mixing bowl, combine the seafood seasoning, salt, mayo, and ¾ cup of the panko breadcrumbs. Mix well. Add the heart of palm, artichoke hearts, mashed chickpeas, and veggies into the mayo mixture. Combine well.

Form 8 patties and set them on a parchment-lined plate or tray. Place into the freezer for 1 hour. This will help ensure they stay together better when cooking.

In a medium bowl, add the ½ cup of panko breadcrumbs. Once the palm cakes are set, remove them from the freezer and coat both sides with the remaining panko.

In the same skillet on medium heat, add a thin layer of avocado oil. The size of your pan will determine how much oil you use. In my pan at home, I use about 2 to 3 tablespoons. Be careful not to add too much, as it may cause the cakes to fall apart. Place the cakes into the pan and cook for 3 to 4 minutes on each side or until golden brown. If working in two batches, carefully wipe the pan clean after the first batch and add another thin layer of oil to cook the remaining palm cakes. When removing from the skillet, be gentle, as these cakes are very delicate. Place them on a paper towel–lined plate to absorb any excess oil.

Serve with lemon wedges and Tartar Sauce.

note

I use two wooden spatulas to help me flip the cakes and to remove them from the pan.

cream of rosé rigatoni

SERVES 3 TO 4

Does anyone else only use their favorite noodles while cooking, or is it just me? I mean, I never stray from bucatini, ziti, lasagna noodles, or rigaTONI, of course haha. The rigatoni noodle is so perfect for this dish because it soaks up all the yummy tomatoey basil goodness. This is such a fun recipe that is bright and delicious for any time of the year. **TP**

3¾ cups water, divided

1½ cups raw cashews

2 tablespoons olive oil

½ cup sliced shallots

4 cloves garlic, minced

½ cup vegan rosé wine

4 large on-the-vine tomatoes, quartered

½ cup freshly chopped basil, plus additional for serving

Kosher salt and freshly ground black pepper

1 (12 to 16-ounce) box rigatoni pasta

¼ teaspoon crushed red pepper flakes, for serving

Freshly squeezed lemon juice and olive oil, for serving

In a medium saucepan, bring 3 cups of water to a boil, then add the cashews. Boil for 2 minutes, then turn down the heat to medium. The water should still be simmering but not a full rolling boil. Let the cashews cook for 30 minutes, or until they are tender. Once done, drain the cashews and rinse with cold water. Then transfer the cashews with the remaining ¾ cup of water in a blender. Blend on high for 30 seconds to 1 minute until smooth. Set aside.

Place the olive oil, shallots, and garlic in a large pot or Dutch oven over medium heat. Sauté for 3 to 4 minutes. Pour in the rosé and cook down for 2 minutes, until evaporated. Add the tomatoes and cook until falling apart, about 6 to 8 minutes. Stir in the ½ cup basil and cook for 1 to 2 minutes.

Carefully add the tomato mixture to the blender and blend until thoroughly combined with the cashews. Pour the sauce back into the pan and simmer for 10 to 15 minutes more, stirring often. Season to taste with salt and pepper.

While the sauce is simmering, cook the pasta per instructions on the package.

Drain the pasta and add to the pan with the sauce; toss well to coat all the noodles. Sprinkle the red pepper flakes over the pasta. Serve with a dash of fresh lemon juice, fresh basil, and olive oil drizzled over the top.

mushroom bourguignon

SERVES 3 TO 4

Hearty and homey, this dish will bring comfort to your taste buds and soul. Perfect for those chilly fall or winter evenings; the only other things you'll need are fuzzy slippers and good company. **TP**

4 tablespoons vegan butter

16 ounces whole baby Bella mushrooms, cleaned and roughly chopped

8 ounces whole white mushrooms, cleaned and roughly chopped

½ large yellow onion, roughly chopped

2 large carrots, peeled and roughly chopped

4 cloves garlic, minced

1 teaspoon fresh thyme leaves

2 tablespoons tomato paste

1½ cups vegan red wine

1½ cups vegetable broth

2 tablespoons cornstarch powder

1 cup frozen peas

Kosher salt and freshly ground black pepper

Mashed potatoes and chopped fresh parsley, for serving

Place the butter, mushrooms, and onion in a Dutch oven or heavy-bottom pot over medium heat. Sauté for 5 to 7 minutes, until the onions are translucent. Add the carrots and sauté for an additional 4 minutes.

Stir in the garlic and thyme. Cook for 1 to 2 minutes, then add the tomato paste. Mix well to combine. Next, pour in the wine, scraping anything off the bottom of the pan using a wooden spoon as the wine cooks down, about 2 to 3 minutes.

In a small bowl, whisk the vegetable broth and cornstarch together to remove any clumps. Pour this into the sauteed veggies. Bring to a boil, then turn down to a simmer until the liquid has thickened, about 10 to 15 minutes. Add the frozen peas and season to taste with salt and pepper.

This is best served over mashed potatoes. Garnish with parsley and serve.

note

To remove thyme leaves from the stem, gently hold the stem and run your thumb and index finger down it.

tofu cutlets

SERVES 3 TO 4

This is a staple in my kitchen. You can use this recipe for almost any dish by just changing a few spices here and there or pairing it with different sauces, using them in your favorite Italian, Asian, or American dishes. It has everything you'd want in a cutlet: flavor, tenderness, and crunch. **TP**

1 (16-ounce) package super-firm tofu, not stored in water

¾ cup all-purpose flour (or any gluten-free flour)

2 tablespoons poultry seasoning

1 tablespoon onion powder

1 tablespoon garlic powder

1 teaspoon kosher salt

1½ cups sparkling water

2 cups panko breadcrumbs (can substitute with gluten-free panko)

Finely grated zest of 1 lemon

Avocado oil, for frying

Open the tofu and rinse with water. Carefully pat the tofu dry with a paper towel or clean tea towel. Then arrange the tofu so that you are horizontal to the longest side. Cut the tofu into 6 to 8 slices, roughly 1-inch wide. Set aside.

In a mixing bowl, place the flour and seasonings, and whisk to combine. Then pour in the sparkling water and whisk until you get a smooth batter. In another mixing bowl, place the panko and lemon zest and whisk together.

Place one piece of tofu into the flour and sparkling water batter, then into the panko and set aside on a plate lined with parchment paper. Be sure to coat well. Repeat until all the tofu is coated. Don't be afraid to press the panko down into the tofu. This will help get those crunchy bits to stick. Gently shake off or remove any excess coating.

In a large, deep-sided skillet over medium-high heat, add about a 1-inch layer of avocado oil and cook the tofu pieces for 4 to 5 minutes. Flip the cutlets throughout cooking until both sides are golden brown. If working in two batches, carefully wipe the pan clean of any oil and panko before adding another 1-inch layer to finish cooking the cutlets.

Remove when cooked and place on a paper towel–lined plate to remove any excess oil.

Slice the cutlets diagonally in half or in multiple slices. Serve in your main dish, with sides, or even on top of a salad.

note

If you cannot find the super-firm tofu, you can use a block of 14-ounce extra-firm tofu. Just be sure to drain and press any excess water out of it first.

shep's pie

SERVES **4** TO **6**

I only just started making this dish about a year ago, and it's quickly become a household staple. The mushrooms are so wonderful and meaty, and the wine adds a beautiful richness to this family-style meal. I'm all about putting a twist on the classics, and I really hope you enjoy this one. And if you're feeling fancy, you can add a handful of shredded vegan parm to your mashed potatoes. **TP**

filling

3 tablespoons olive oil

1 medium yellow onion, finely diced

16 ounces baby Bella mushrooms, cleaned and finely chopped

16 ounces white mushrooms, cleaned and finely chopped

1 cup carrots, peeled and finely diced

6 cloves garlic, minced

2 teaspoons chopped fresh rosemary

¾ cup vegan red wine (I use pinot noir)

2 tablespoons vegan and gluten-free Worcestershire sauce or tamari

3 tablespoons tomato paste

1 cup frozen peas

2 teaspoons kosher salt

Freshly ground black pepper

mashed potatoes

6 large russet potatoes, peeled, washed, and cubed

1 cup vegan butter

3 tablespoons unsweetened plant-based milk

Kosher salt and freshly ground black pepper

Vegan cheese, chopped chives, or vegan sour cream, for garnish

tip

Sometimes I like to mash shredded vegan parmesan cheese into my potatoes to give them a little extra something special. Also, you can broil the Shep's Pie for the last 1 to 2 minutes to get a nice golden color.

Continued

Preheat the oven to 375°F.

To make the filling, place the olive oil and onions in a large skillet or Dutch oven over medium heat. Sauté for 3 to 5 minutes, then add both types of mushrooms. Allow the mushrooms to cook down, about 5 to 7 minutes. The mushrooms will cook down significantly. Then add the carrots and sauté for 4 more minutes. Add the garlic and rosemary and sauté for 1 minute, until fragrant.

Pour in the wine and allow to cook down for 2 to 3 minutes, scraping any bits off the bottom of the pan using a wooden spoon. Pour in the Worcestershire sauce and tomato paste. Mix thoroughly to incorporate everything. Lower the heat to a simmer and add the frozen peas. Season with salt and pepper to taste.

While the filling is simmering, make the mashed potatoes. Fill a Dutch oven or heavy-bottom pot with water and bring to a boil. Add the potatoes and boil for about 7 to 10 minutes, until tender. Turn off the heat and strain the potatoes. Place them back into the same pot, add the butter, and mash until all lumps are removed. Pour in the desired amount of milk and mash again. Season with salt and pepper to taste.

Add the filling to a 9 by 13-inch rectangular baking dish. Spread the mashed potatoes over the top of the filling and bake for 20 to 25 minutes.

Allow to cool for at least 5 minutes before serving. Serve with vegan cheese, chopped chives, or vegan sour cream (Forager is my favorite) for topping.

note

If using a Dutch oven for the filling, you could just add mashed potatoes to the top and place into the oven to bake.

the after-

party

Chokladbollar
(Swedish Chocolate balls)

MAKES **16** BALLS

Chokladbollar translates to "chocolate balls" in Swedish. The chocolate no-bake morsels are a popular treat in Sweden, often enjoyed with a midmorning or late-afternoon cup of coffee. I've replaced almost all the granulated sugar with dates, adding fiber and antioxidants. I like to make my balls on the small side and take them with me for a little boost of energy before or after workouts. **AR**

1 cup gluten-free old-fashioned rolled oats

5 tablespoons vegan butter, chilled

10 pitted Medjool dates

2 tablespoons unsweetened cocoa powder

½ teaspoon pure vanilla extract

1 tablespoon granulated sugar

Pinch of table salt

Unsweetened shredded coconut, for rolling the balls in

Place the oats in a food processor and pulse until they resemble coarse flour. Add the butter, dates, cocoa powder, vanilla, sugar, and salt. Blend, scraping down the sides of the processor as needed, until everything is well combined and the dough sticks together when pressed.

Roll the dough into balls roughly 1 inch in diameter and set on a plate. Then roll each ball in shredded coconut. Refrigerate in a sealed container for at least 30 minutes before serving. Store in a sealed container in the fridge for up to 5 days.

lemon bundt

SERVES 6 TO 8

This is one of my grandpa's favorites, and I know that when he likes something, it must be good! I always try to impress him with dishes because he is the official taste tester. If Grandpa approves, everyone approves. **TP**

cake

Nonstick cooking spray, for greasing the Bundt pan

2 cups all-purpose flour

1 teaspoon baking powder

1 teaspoon baking soda

1 cup cane sugar

½ teaspoon kosher salt

Finely grated zest of 1 lemon

½ cup olive oil

1 teaspoon pure vanilla extract

1 cup vegan vanilla yogurt (I use Silk soy yogurt)

Freshly squeezed juice of 2 lemons

icing

1½ cups confectioners' sugar

1 tablespoon water

1 to 2 tablespoons freshly squeezed lemon juice

½ teaspoon pure vanilla extract

Preheat the oven to 350°F. Spray a Bundt pan with nonstick cooking spray and set aside.

Place the flour, baking powder, baking soda, cane sugar, salt, and lemon zest in a large mixing bowl. Mix to combine everything with a wooden spoon. Add the olive oil, vanilla extract, 2 tablespoons water, yogurt, and lemon juice. Using the same wooden spoon, stir to combine, removing all the lumps. Pour the batter into the prepared Bundt pan and place on a baking sheet.

Bake for 40 to 45 minutes, or until a fork comes out clean.

While the cake is baking, prepare the icing by combining all the icing ingredients in a medium bowl. Using a hand mixer, mix to make a silky icing. Once the cake is done, let it cool in the refrigerator. When the pan is cool enough to handle, remove the cake from the pan onto a cake stand or serving tray. Drizzle the icing over the top, slice, and serve. Cover with plastic wrap; it will keep for up to 5 days.

dark chocolate–coconut bars

MAKES **16** BARS

If you like chocolate and coconut, these bars are for you! Make these ahead of time, as they need to set in the freezer for at least 1 hour. **AR**

- 3 cups unsweetened shredded coconut, plus extra for garnish
- ⅔ cup canned coconut milk (scoop off the solid thick cream from the top of the can before adding the liquid)
- 2 tablespoons coconut oil
- 1 teaspoon pure vanilla extract
- 3 tablespoons maple syrup
- 7 ounces (200 grams) dairy-free dark chocolate (I like to use 75 percent cacao)

Line an 8 by 8-inch baking dish with parchment paper.

Place the coconut, coconut milk, coconut oil, vanilla, and maple syrup into a food processor and blend until smooth. Scrape down the sides as needed. Spread the mixture into the prepared baking dish and freeze for at least 1 hour.

Slice the frozen mixture into 16 equal squares. Remove the bars from the baking dish.

Line a small baking sheet with parchment paper. Melt the dark chocolate using a double boiler or by microwaving in a deep bowl at 20-second intervals, stirring it between each interval. Dunk a bar into the chocolate and coat it completely using a spoon or tongs. Place the bar onto the baking sheet. Repeat with the remaining bars. Return to the freezer for 10 minutes to harden the chocolate.

Allow the bars to thaw for at least 5 minutes before serving. Garnish with additional coconut. Store leftover bars in an airtight container in the fridge for up to 5 days or in the freezer for up to 2 weeks.

key lime mini cheesecakes

MAKES **12** MINI CHEESECAKES

No dairy, no problem! You won't believe how rich and creamy this no-bake dessert is. We love a buttery graham cracker crust, and the ratio of crust to filling certainly reflects that. But it won't stop you from enjoying the beautiful freshness of the key lime. The cashews need to soak for at least 30 minutes, and the cheesecakes need a few hours in the freezer, so I recommend making this dessert a day before you plan to serve it. **AR**

Nonstick cooking spray, for greasing the muffin tin

1½ cups raw cashews

1½ cups graham cracker crumbs (about 10 graham cracker sheets)

5 tablespoons vegan butter, melted

¼ cup freshly squeezed key lime juice

⅓ cup melted coconut oil

⅔ cup canned coconut milk (use all the solid cream before adding the liquid)

½ cup maple syrup

1 tablespoon finely grated key lime zest

Using the nonstick spray, grease a 12-cup muffin tin. This is a key step!

Place the cashews into a small bowl or jar and cover them completely with boiling water. Allow them to soak for at least 30 minutes.

Add the graham cracker crumbs and butter to a medium bowl. Stir to combine. Spoon the coated crumbs evenly into the muffin tin. Press down on the crumbs using the back of a ¼-cup measuring cup or the bottom of a glass to firmly pack them down into each slot. Place the muffin tin in the freezer.

Drain the cashews and add them to a food processor or blender along with the lime juice, coconut oil, coconut milk, and maple syrup. Blend until smooth.

Remove the muffin tin from the freezer and divide the filling among the slots. Smooth down the tops using the back of a spoon. Sprinkle a bit of zest over each cheesecake. Cover the tin with plastic wrap and return it to the freezer for at least 4 hours, or until the cheesecakes have hardened.

When ready to serve, allow the cheesecakes to thaw for about 10 minutes before popping them out of the muffin tin. Leftover cheesecakes can be stored in an airtight container in the freezer for up to 2 weeks.

chocolate sheet cake

SERVES **15** TO **18**; MAKES ONE (12 BY 18-INCH) CAKE

We like to call this our showstopper, the ultimate party cake. This dessert will have all you chocolate lovers out there swooning. Nobody will ever guess that there is an entire block of tofu blended into the batter, and what's better than sneaking protein into a super-yummy dessert? While we have been known to bake this gigantic cake for just the two of us (no regrets!), this recipe is easy to cut in half; just use a 9 by 13-inch baking pan instead. **TP**

cake

Nonstick cooking spray, for greasing the baking pan

2 cups vegan butter

2 cups water

½ cup unsweetened cocoa powder

1 cup oat milk

2 teaspoons apple cider vinegar

1 (14-ounce) block firm tofu

2 cups cane sugar

1 cup firmly packed dark-brown sugar

4 cups all-purpose flour

2 teaspoons baking soda

2 teaspoons ground cinnamon

1 teaspoon kosher salt

4 teaspoons pure vanilla extract

frosting

1 cup vegan butter

½ cup unsweetened cocoa powder

1 teaspoon pure vanilla extract

7 to 8 cups confectioners' sugar

5 to 6 tablespoons oat milk

Chopped pecans or walnuts, for garnish

───────────────

Preheat the oven to 350°F. Spray a 12 by 18-inch baking pan with nonstick cooking spray.

To make the cake, place the butter in a medium saucepan over medium heat. Once the butter is melted, add the water and cocoa powder. Whisk until smooth. Turn off the heat and set aside.

In a small bowl, mix the oat milk and apple cider vinegar together. Set aside.

Using a food processor or high-speed blender, whip the tofu until creamy. Set aside.

Place both sugars in a large mixing bowl. Sift in the flour, baking soda, cinnamon, and salt. Pour in the chocolate mixture, milk, creamed tofu, and vanilla. Mix well to combine. Pour the cake batter in the prepared pan. Bake for 20 to 25 minutes, until a toothpick comes out of the center clean.

While the cake is baking, prepare the frosting. Place the butter in the same medium saucepan over medium heat. Once melted, whisk in the cocoa powder and vanilla. Turn off the heat and set the frosting aside.

In a large mixing bowl, add the confectioners' sugar, butter mixture, and milk. Mix together until you get a smooth frosting. Once the cake is done baking, immediately pour the frosting over the cake. Sprinkle the nuts over the top, if using. Let the cake cool before serving. Store covered in plastic wrap for up to 5 days.

carrot cake

My parents' wedding cake was a carrot cake, and they eat it every year on their anniversary, so Toni was under a lot of pressure to make a vegan version that would win them over. She nailed it. From the freshly grated carrots and crunchy walnuts in the wonderfully moist cake to the flaky coconut in the mindblowing cream cheese frosting, this is a dessert that is seriously hard to stop eating. If you are Team Raisins, you can throw those in, or you can take out the walnuts for a nut-free version. **AR**

cake

Nonstick cooking spray, for greasing the cake pan

¾ unsweetened plant-based milk (we use almond milk)

1 tablespoon apple cider vinegar

2 cups gluten-free flour (we use King Arthur)

1 teaspoon baking soda

1 teaspoon baking powder

1 teaspoon kosher salt

2 teaspoons ground cinnamon

¼ teaspoon ground nutmeg

1 cup firmly packed light- or dark-brown sugar

1 cup cane sugar

¾ cup vegan sour cream

¾ cup canola oil

2 teaspoons pure vanilla extract

2 cups peeled, washed, and finely shredded carrots

1 cup chopped walnuts

frosting

½ cup vegan cream cheese

½ cup vegan butter, softened

4 cups confectioners' sugar

½ cup unsweetened shredded coconut (the bigger the shreds, the better)

1 teaspoon pure vanilla extract

Splash of unsweetened plant-based milk

Continued

Preheat the oven to 350°F. Spray a rectangular 9 by 13-inch or two round 8-inch cake pans with nonstick cooking spray.

To make the cake, mix the milk and apple cider vinegar together in a small bowl and set aside.

In a large mixing bowl, sift together the flour, baking soda, baking powder, salt, cinnamon, and nutmeg. Add in both sugars and stir well. In the same mixing bowl, add the sour cream, oil, vanilla, and milk mixture. Mix well to combine, then stir in the carrots and walnuts.

Pour the cake batter into the prepared pan. Bake for 30 to 35 minutes if using a rectangular pan. If using two round pans, bake for 25 minutes, until a toothpick comes out clean.

While the cake is baking, prepare the frosting. In a large mixing bowl, cream together the cream cheese and butter using a hand mixer. Add in the confectioners' sugar a little at a time until it's all incorporated. Add the shredded coconut, vanilla, and milk until your desired consistency is reached.

When the cake is cool, spread the frosting over the top of the cake before serving. For a two-layer cake, cover the first layer in frosting, then place the second layer on top. Completely cover the entire cake, including the sides. Chill in the fridge for about an hour before serving. Store with plastic wrap covering the cut edge of the cake in the fridge. This will keep for 5 days.

peanut caramel candy bars

MAKES 16 SMALL BARS

If you want to impress someone with a homemade healthy dessert (also gluten-free!), you've come to the right place. Using only natural ingredients, this treat is sweetened with dates and maple syrup instead of the corn syrup, refined sugar, and artificial flavorings of traditional candy bars. Cutting into the bars and seeing the layers is so satisfying, and that sprinkle of sea salt on top enhances the delicious flavors in just the right way. Make sure your dates are nice and soft, since they play a key role! **AR**

Nonstick cooking spray, for greasing the baking dish

1 cup roasted and salted peanuts

20 pitted Medjool dates, divided

½ teaspoon pure vanilla extract, divided

¾ cup unsweetened and unsalted creamy peanut butter

½ cup melted coconut oil, divided

4 tablespoons unsweetened cocoa powder

1 teaspoon maple syrup

Flaky sea salt

Line an 8 by 8-inch baking dish with parchment paper. (Greasing the bottom of the baking dish first with nonstick spray can help keep the parchment paper in place.)

Place the peanuts, 10 of the dates, and ¼ teaspoon of the vanilla into a food processor. Blend on high speed until the mixture is crumbly but sticks together when pressed, about one minute. Press the mixture into the bottom of the lined baking dish to form an even layer. Place the baking dish into the freezer.

Now add the peanut butter, the 10 remaining dates, ¼ cup of the coconut oil, and the remaining ¼ teaspoon of vanilla to the food processor. Blend on high speed until smooth, scraping down the sides of the food processor as necessary. Take the baking dish out of the freezer and spread the mixture over the base layer. Return the dish to the freezer.

Continued

Pour the remaining ¼ cup of coconut oil into a small pot. Add the cocoa powder and maple syrup. Whisk well over low heat for about 1 to 2 minutes until combined. Remove the baking dish from the freezer and pour the liquid mixture over the second layer. Tilt the dish in all directions to make sure the mixture coats the entire second layer evenly. Top with a sprinkle of sea salt. Return to the freezer until the chocolate layer is solid, at least 15 minutes.

When ready to serve, remove the bars from the freezer and allow them to thaw for 5 minutes. Run the blade of a sharp knife under hot water. Cut the bars into 16 squares and serve.

Store the bars in an airtight container in the fridge for up to 5 days or in the freezer for up to 3 months. If frozen, allow time for them to thaw before serving (this can take up to 20 minutes).

oatmeal cookies

MAKES **18** TO **24** COOKIES

By adding a hint of cocoa to these cookies, you will have your guests guessing what that special ingredient is. To share the secret or to not share the secret? That is the question. **TP**

1 cup vegan butter, softened

1½ cups firmly packed dark-brown sugar

1 flax egg (page x)

1 tablespoon maple syrup

2 teaspoons pure vanilla extract

1 teaspoon ground cinnamon

1 teaspoon unsweetened cocoa powder

2 cups old-fashioned rolled oats

1½ cups all-purpose flour

1 teaspoon baking soda

½ teaspoon baking powder

NF

Preheat the oven to 350°F.

In a large mixing bowl, cream together the butter and sugar using a hand mixer.

Add the flax egg, maple syrup, vanilla, cinnamon, and cocoa powder. Mix well. Pour in the oats and stir.

Sift the flour, baking powder, and baking soda into the batter. Mix until combined.

Roll enough dough to form the shape of a golf ball, or just slightly bigger, and place onto a parchment-lined baking sheet. You should be able to fit 12 balls onto the sheet. Repeat this step until the dough is gone.

Bake for 8 to 10 minutes, until light brown. Store in an airtight container for 1 week.

feeling

saucy

Left to right: Maple Tahini Dressing (page 112), Ranch Dressing (page 111), Orange Vinaigrette (page 113)

ranch dressing*

MAKES 1 CUP

To me, ranch is the perfect dressing or dip, since it goes with just about everything. By adding fresh herbs, we think this homemade recipe is a sophisticated level-up from the ranch dressings you can buy at the store. **TP**

1 cup vegan mayonnaise

¼ cup unsweetened almond milk

1 tablespoon chopped fresh parsley

1 tablespoon chopped fresh dill

1 tablespoon chopped fresh chives

1 teaspoon minced garlic

1 teaspoon onion powder

½ teaspoon kosher salt

Freshly ground black pepper

Mix all the ingredients together in a small bowl. Season to taste with more salt and pepper if needed. Refrigerate for 20 minutes before serving. This will keep refrigerated for up to 5 days, but it won't last that long!

maple tahini dressing

MAKES ABOUT ⅔ CUP

The bold flavors of mustard, maple syrup, and lemon juice combine with the mild and nutty tahini to create a beautifully balanced creamy, dreamy dressing. It will elevate any veggie or salad, but we think it pairs best with our Peach Kale Salad (page 44). **AR**

⅓ cup tahini

½ tablespoon Dijon mustard

2 tablespoons maple syrup

2 tablespoons freshly squeezed lemon juice

Pinch of kosher salt

¼ cup water

Whisk together the tahini, mustard, maple syrup, lemon juice, and salt in a small bowl. Add water, 1 tablespoon at a time, and continue to whisk until smooth. I like my dressing thick but pourable. Continue to add a little bit of water at a time until you reach your desired consistency. Drizzle over salad, vegetables, bowls, or serve with falafel or fritters. Store in a sealed jar in the fridge for up to 5 days.

orange vinaigrette

MAKES ABOUT ¾ CUP DRESSING

This easy dressing uses the simple yet effective combination of sweetness (orange and maple syrup) and tang (mustard and vinegar) to brighten up any salad. I always have a jar of this vinaigrette on hand in the fridge. **AR**

Finely grated zest of 1 orange

⅓ cup freshly squeezed orange juice

¼ cup extra-virgin olive oil

1 tablespoon maple syrup

1 tablespoon Dijon mustard

1 tablespoon apple cider vinegar

¼ teaspoon table salt, plus additional as needed

Freshly ground black pepper

Whisk all of the ingredients together in a small bowl. Season to taste with more salt and pepper as needed. Serve with our Shredded Brussels Sprouts Salad (page 41). This dressing can be served chilled or at room temperature. Store in a sealed jar in the fridge for up to 1 week. Shake well before serving.

garlicky lemon aioli

MAKES 1 CUP

I love garlic and I love lemon; both of them combined is a perfect partnership! You can use this sauce for a variety of things, such as our Heart of Palm Calamari (page 37), Heart of Palm Cakes (page 82), or our TLT (page 68). **TP**

1 cup vegan mayonnaise

Freshly squeezed juice of
½ lemon

2 cloves garlic, minced

Kosher salt and freshly ground
black pepper

Mix all the ingredients together in a small bowl. Let this marinate in the refrigerator for 20 minutes before using as a spread or dip. Store in an airtight container in the fridge for up to 3 days.

tartar sauce

MAKES ABOUT ½ CUP

This sauce is bold and bright! It has tang and a sneaky sweetness from the relish. Pair this with our Heart of Palm Cakes (page 82) or Heart of Palm Calamari (page 37). **TP**

½ cup vegan mayonnaise

2 teaspoons Dijon mustard

1 tablespoon freshly squeezed
lemon juice

1 tablespoon chopped fresh dill

2 tablespoons sweet relish

Kosher salt and freshly ground
black pepper

Combine all the ingredients in a small bowl and mix well. Season with salt and pepper to taste. Store in an airtight container in the fridge for up to 3 days.

Left to right: Tartar Sauce (page 114), Garlicky Lemon Aioli (page 114)

peanut dressing*

MAKES ABOUT 1½ CUPS

This creamy, nutty dressing is serving you tang, saltiness, and sweetness, with just a hint of spice. It's perfect for a crunchy salad like our Thai Salad (page 46), but it can also be used as a sauce poured over noodles or stir-fried veggies. **TP**

¾ cup creamy natural peanut or almond butter

¼ cup rice vinegar

⅓ cup tamari

4 tablespoons agave nectar

1 clove garlic, minced

1 teaspoon peeled and grated fresh ginger

¼ teaspoon crushed red pepper flakes

2 tablespoons water

In a medium bowl, whisk all the ingredients together until combined. Store, covered, in the refrigerator for up to 5 days.

hoisin peanut sauce

MAKES ALMOST **1** CUP, DEPENDING ON HOW MUCH WATER YOU ADD

I think of hoisin as the Chinese barbecue sauce. Made with fermented soybean paste, it is sweet, salty, and umami. It has a unique and strong taste, so one way I like to introduce it to friends is by mixing it with peanut butter and garlic to make this lovely dipping sauce. I add it to my noodles or stir-fry, or I dip my protein, like our Crispy Tofu Nuggets (page 34), in it. **AR**

½ cup creamy unsweetened peanut butter

3 tablespoons hoisin sauce

2 tablespoons freshly squeezed lime juice

4 teaspoons soy sauce

2 teaspoons sriracha, chili garlic sauce, or sambal oelek

1 clove garlic, minced

Warm water, as needed

In a small bowl, whisk together the peanut butter, hoisin sauce, lime juice, soy sauce, sriracha, and garlic. Add 1 tablespoon of warm water at a time until smooth and slightly runny. Store in an airtight jar in the fridge for up to 3 days.

Left to right: Sweet and Spicy Mayo (page 118), Hoisin Peanut Sauce (page 117), Sesame Soy Mayo (page 118)

sesame soy mayo

It's so nice when some simple additions can totally transform an ingredient. Vegan mayonnaise, also known as "vegenaise" or "vegan dressing and spread," is a basic spread that certainly deserves a spot in your fridge. But with some umami and spice mixed in, it goes from basic to WOW. Try this sauce drizzled over rice or served alongside Crispy Tofu Nuggets (page 34). **AR**

½ cup vegan mayonnaise

1 teaspoon tamari

½ teaspoon toasted sesame oil

¼ to ½ teaspoon sriracha

1 teaspoon toasted sesame seeds

Combine the mayonnaise, tamari, and sesame oil in a small bowl. Add the sriracha to taste. Stir in the sesame seeds. The longer you let it sit before serving, the more flavorful the mayo will be. Store in an airtight jar in the fridge for up to 1 week.

sweet and spicy mayo

MAKES 1 CUP

Have you ever wanted to pour a sauce over everything? Well, this is that sauce for me! A super-delicious sauce that seriously goes well on anything. Spread it on a wrap, add it to rice, or pair it with our Coconut Cauliflower Tacos (page 71). **TP**

¾ cup vegan mayonnaise

2 tablespoons sriracha sauce

1 to 2 tablespoons sweet chili sauce

1 clove garlic, minced

Juice of ½ lime

Mix all ingredients together in a bowl. Refrigerate for 20 minutes before serving. Store in an airtight jar in the fridge for up to 1 week.

shaking

things up

iced matcha latte

SERVES 1

When I need a break from coffee, this is my absolute go-to. So easy to make, everyone will think you're the new hottest barista in town. Not only does matcha have great health benefits, but this superfood's antioxidants may aid in recovery after intense training. I like to use the Barista version of oat milk to make for a creamier and frothier latte. **TP**

¼ cup water

1 teaspoon matcha powder

2 teaspoons agave nectar

¼ to ½ cup ice

¾ cup barista oat milk

Using a blender or handheld frother, blend the water, matcha powder, and agave together.

In your cup or glass of choice, add the ice, then pour the matcha mix over it. Last, pour in the oat milk and give it a gentle stir. Serve with a metal straw, if you like, and enjoy.

You can also froth the oat milk too if you'd like!

healthy hot chocolate

SERVES 1

This deliciously rich and chocolaty drink takes about 5 minutes to make. You won't believe it's dairy-free and naturally sweetened. I like using unsweetened roasted almond milk to give this hot chocolate an even creamier feel. **AR**

1 cup plant-based milk

2 tablespoons unsweetened cocoa powder

2 pitted Medjool dates

1 tablespoon almond butter (can omit for nut-free version)

1 teaspoon pure vanilla extract

Heat the milk in a small saucepan over low heat.

Add the remaining ingredients and whisk to combine. Simmer on low heat for 5 minutes or until the dates are soft and the temperature is to your liking.

Carefully pour the mixture into a blender. Blend on high until smooth and frothy. Pour into a warmed mug and enjoy immediately.

golden milk

SERVES 1

I don't drink coffee, but I really enjoy a warming drink, especially when I'm spending time in Sweden! Turmeric contains curcumin, which has been shown to have anti-inflammatory properties, aid in digestion, and promote brain function. Black pepper may seem like an unusual addition, but it helps the body absorb the turmeric and combines nicely with the cinnamon and ginger. Sometimes I use maple syrup and sometimes I don't—I recommend trying it both ways. **AR**

1 cup plant-based milk (I usually use oat milk or almond milk)

½ teaspoon ground turmeric

½ teaspoon ground cinnamon

¼ teaspoon ground ginger

¼ teaspoon cayenne pepper

1 teaspoon maple syrup, optional

Freshly ground black pepper

Add the milk, turmeric, cinnamon, ginger, and cayenne pepper to a blender. Add the maple syrup, if using. Grind some black pepper in and blend on high until smooth and frothy.

Pour the mixture into a small saucepan over low-medium heat; be careful not to allow it to come to a boil. Warm to your desired temperature. Carefully pour into a mug and enjoy immediately.

pro tip

The pigment in turmeric stains pretty much everything, so be careful when measuring and pouring, and rinse out your cup immediately after finishing your Golden Milk.

blended green juice

SERVES 2

Store-bought fresh-pressed juices can be expensive, especially considering they are just fruits and veggies. But good juicers can be expensive as well, and we don't all have the counter space or storage for a big appliance. This pretty and hydrating green juice recipe is made using a blender and a sieve. The finer the sieve, the less pulp in your juice. **AR**

3 stalks celery, roughly chopped

2 cups firmly packed fresh spinach

2 green apples, cored and roughly chopped

1 cucumber, roughly chopped

1 tablespoon peeled and roughly chopped fresh ginger

¼ cup freshly squeezed lemon juice

1 cup cold water

Ice

Add all the ingredients, except the ice, to a blender and blend on high until the mixture reaches the consistency of a smoothie. Place a fine-mesh sieve over a large bowl and slowly pour the blended juice through the sieve. Use a rubber spatula or large spoon to mix around and press down the pulp, ensuring that all the liquid strains into the bowl.

Compost the pulp or save it for a smoothie, muffin, or veggie burger recipe.

To serve, fill two tall glasses with ice and divide the juice evenly between the glasses.

peanut butter shake

SERVES 1

This creamy shake tastes like something you could order at a diner but is only made with clean and healthy ingredients. Cacao nibs add a subtle chocolaty flavor and a delightful crunch. **AR**

1 cup plant-based milk (I think almond milk pairs well with the peanut butter)

1 banana

2 tablespoons unsweetened peanut butter

1 tablespoon raw cacao nibs, plus additional for garnish

2 dates

Pinch of kosher salt

Add all the ingredients to a blender and blend on high until smooth. Serve in a 10-ounce tall glass topped with an additional sprinkle of cacao nibs.

strawberry–banana smoothie

SERVES 1

The best way to sneak veg into your breakfast! Frozen cauliflower has a neutral flavor and gives this smoothie a nice thick consistency. The orange-strawberry-banana combo makes me feel like I'm on a tropical vacation, but you can add cauliflower to any smoothie recipe for some extra fiber and B-vitamins; just keep in mind you might need to add more liquid so everything blends up nicely. **AR**

1 cup freshly squeezed orange juice

½ banana

3 florets frozen cauliflower

½ cup frozen strawberries (about 5 strawberries)

Dash of fresh lime juice

Fresh orange slice, for garnish

Add all the ingredients to a blender and blend on high until smooth. Serve in a tall glass with an orange slice or in a portable mug to take on the road.

spicy grapefruit margarita

SERVES 1

This is the easiest and fastest way to get a sweet, tangy, and spicy margarita. No infusion or simple syrup required! Grapefruit is one of the healthiest citrus fruits out there, and it gives this marg a pretty pink hue. You can make your cocktail spicier by adjusting the number of jalapeño coins. If you are really brave, leave the seeds in! **AR**

1 lime wedge

Margarita salt, to rim the glass

3 jalapeño coins, seeds removed, divided

2 ounces white tequila

2 ounces freshly squeezed grapefruit juice

1 ounce freshly squeezed lime juice

1 ounce agave nectar

Ice for shaker and glass

Rub the rim of your margarita glass with a lime wedge and dip the rim into the margarita salt to coat. Set the glass aside.

Add two of the jalapeño coins to a shaker and gently muddle them. Add the tequila, grapefruit juice, lime juice, agave, and a scoop of ice to the shaker and shake until chilled.

Place fresh ice into your glass and strain the mixture over the ice. Add the remaining third jalapeño coin for garnish.

kombucha mule

SERVES 1

Adding alcohol to the probiotic-rich fermented tea drink to make our version of a Moscow Mule: we call it retox while you detox. Serve in a copper mug for that classic feel. **AR**

½ ounce freshly squeezed lime juice

1½ ounces vodka

Ice to fill mug

4 ounces ginger-flavored kombucha

1 lime wedge, for garnish

Add the lime juice and vodka to a copper mug or short glass. Fill the mug or glass with ice and pour the kombucha over the ice. Stir to combine and drop in a lime wedge for garnish.

tip

Finding vegan cocktails isn't hard, since almost every brand of hard liquor is vegan. However, many fizzes or sours are shaken with egg white to give them a fun layer of silky froth that looks so fancy. Enter chickpea juice, otherwise known as aquafaba. This is the liquid that canned chickpeas sit in. So next time you make a recipe with chickpeas, set aside that starchy liquid and use it to make one of our favorite cocktails.

rosemary gin fizz

SERVES 1

The herb and citrus flavors pair together so nicely in this beautiful cocktail. There is no need to take time to infuse your gin when shaking it up with a rosemary sprig does the trick! **AR**

Ice for the glass and shaker

2 ounces gin

1 ounce freshly squeezed lemon juice

¾ ounce agave syrup

2 sprigs fresh rosemary, divided

2 tablespoons aquafaba (page viii)

1 ounce club soda

1 lemon slice, for garnish

Chill a coupe glass by putting a few ice cubes into it and setting aside.

Add the gin, lemon juice, agave, 1 rosemary sprig, and the aquafaba to a shaker without ice. This is called dry shaking. Shake vigorously for 15 seconds. Add a handful of ice and shake again until the outside of the shaker is very cold.

Discard the ice from your glass and strain the drink into your glass. Top with club soda and garnish with the remaining rosemary sprig and the lemon slice.

whiskey sour

SERVES 1

Can you tell we love lemon? A whiskey sour is bright and warming with its balance of citrus, sweetener, and spirits. Nobody will believe that the gorgeous layer of foam on top is made from chickpea liquid! Angostura bitters add dimension (and look cool!) but don't worry if you don't have them at home. **AR**

2 ounces bourbon

¾ ounce freshly squeezed lemon juice

½ ounce agave syrup

2 tablespoons aquafaba (page viii)

Ice for shaker and glass

Angostura bitters, optional

Combine the bourbon, lemon juice, agave syrup, and aquafaba in a shaker and dry shake (without ice) for 15 seconds. Fill the shaker with ice and shake again until the outside of the shaker is very cold.

Strain the cocktail into the glass and top with 3 or 4 drops of bitters, if desired.

acknowledgments

Girls Gone Veg would not exist if it weren't for the belief and support of Jonna Humphries-Valente and Sam Finnegan. We look forward to working on many more projects together!

A very special thank-you to Jeremy Reper, Duda Pavao, and Julie Miller-Schuette for the countless things you've helped us with. Thank you to the team at Andrews McMeel Universal, Steve Troha, and Katherine Odom-Tomchin. We are truly grateful.

From Toni:

I would like to express my deepest love and gratitude to my family. Thank you for believing in me. To my mom, Diane, thank you for always being my rock and guiding me in life. To my grandparents, Bob and Wendy, thank you for unwavering support in anything I do and being my most important taste-testers. Because of you all, cooking has become something I truly love and have so much fun doing. Some of my favorite memories are in the kitchen with all of you.

Thank you to all of my dearest friends for your encouragement and kind words throughout this book-making process. Your love and friendship is something I cherish deeply.

Orian, you make me believe I can do anything I set my mind to. From being my best food critic to my sous-chef, your partnership, love, and support have made so much of this possible. I am so grateful for you.

Most importantly, Ali, thank you for joining me on this amazing adventure and making me better every step of the way. My life is so much better with you in it and I'm so lucky to call my best friend, my sister, and my ride-or-die.

From Ali:

Thank you to TDP for being my bestie and business partner. I'm so grateful to you for teaching me about the benefits and joys of plant-based food. I'll never forget our first-ever conversation on the field and knowing right away that you would become one of my favorite people.

Lucas, your endless support and patience made this book possible. Thank you for tasting all of my creations, even when I know you desperately wanted meat for dinner.

To my parents: Bev, the hostess with the mostess, thank you for being on this journey with me every step of the way. I will never have your talent in the kitchen, but I'm so happy that we share this love of food, cooking, and hosting dinner parties. And JR, because of you I have always felt that no dream is too big. Thank you for being my first coach in soccer and in life.

about the authors

Ali Riley was born and raised in Los Angeles, but soccer has taken her all over the world. She currently captains the New Zealand National Team and has represented New Zealand at four FIFA World Cups and four Olympic Games. After leading Stanford University to a national championship game appearance, Ali was drafted in 2010 to play professionally in the U.S. and has since represented three clubs in Europe.

She played for FC Rosengård in Sweden, Chelsea FC in England, and FC Bayern in Germany before returning stateside to play for the Orlando Pride. In 2022, she moved home to Los Angeles and was named captain of Angel City Football Club. She's a five-time New Zealand Player of the Year and was twice nominated for the FIFPRO World XI. Ali is a certified health coach and has a passion for all things food.

In 2017, she launched a business called Love2Eat2Love, posting her healthy recipes on social media and sharing her nutrition expertise with schools and youth soccer clubs. She's a self-proclaimed "flexitarian" who was motivated to eat less meat after learning about how negatively it affects the planet. She soon realized that avoiding animal products also helped her body prepare for and recover after games. Ali is excited to share her best creations and show how easy and fun vegan recipes can be.

Toni Deion Pressley is an American professional soccer player who is native to Melbourne, Florida. After playing collegiate soccer at Florida State University, Toni has been lucky enough to have been a professional soccer player for more than eleven years. She previously played for the Western New York Flash, Washington Spirit, Houston Dash, and Orlando Pride of the NWSL. She currently plays for Breidablik in Iceland. Toni has also played overseas at Ryazan VDV in the Russian Women's Football Championship league and Canberra United in Australia.

Pressley played for various United States national youth teams and was a member of the United States women's national under-twenty and under-twenty-three soccer teams.

Toni also coaches youth soccer and holds her USSF B-License in coaching. She loves teaching youths about soccer and believes in the lessons sports can teach players about themselves and life. Her goal is to make better soccer players, but above all else, better humans.

In 2019, Toni was diagnosed with breast cancer after getting a checkup at the recommendation of the team nutritionist. She successfully underwent surgery and returned to play in the Orlando Pride's final game of the 2019 season.

Toni has been following a vegan diet since 2016 and fully believes in the amazing health benefits associated with this diet. Animal welfare is also very important to Toni; this has largely impacted her decision to make veganism a lifestyle. Toni is eager to share the wonders of a vegan diet that have a fun spin on classic recipes.

metric conversions and equivalents

approximate metric equivalents

Volume

¼ teaspoon	1 milliliter
½ teaspoon	2.5 milliliters
¾ teaspoon	4 milliliters
1 teaspoon	5 milliliters
1¼ teaspoons	6 milliliters
1½ teaspoons	7.5 milliliters
1¾ teaspoons	8.5 milliliters
2 teaspoons	10 milliliters
1 tablespoon (½ fluid ounce)	15 milliliters
2 tablespoons (1 fluid ounce)	30 milliliters
¼ cup	60 milliliters
⅓ cup	80 milliliters
½ cup (4 fluid ounces)	120 milliliters
⅔ cup	160 milliliters
¾ cup	180 milliliters
1 cup (8 fluid ounces)	240 milliliters
1¼ cups	300 milliliters
1½ cups (12 fluid ounces)	360 milliliters
1⅔ cups	400 milliliters
2 cups (1 pint)	460 milliliters
3 cups	700 milliliters
4 cups (1 quart)	.95 liter
1 quart plus ¼ cup	1 liter
4 quarts (1 gallon)	3.8 liters

Weight

¼ ounce	7 grams
½ ounce	14 grams
¾ ounce	21 grams
1 ounce	28 grams
1¼ ounces	35 grams
1½ ounces	42.5 grams
1⅔ ounces	45 grams
2 ounces	57 grams
3 ounces	85 grams
4 ounces (¼ pound)	113 grams
5 ounces	142 grams
6 ounces	170 grams
7 ounces	198 grams
8 ounces (½ pound)	227 grams
16 ounces (1 pound)	454 grams
35.25 ounces (2.2 pounds)	1 kilogram

Length

⅛ inch	3 millimeters
¼ inch	6 millimeters
½ inch	1¼ centimeters
1 inch	2½ centimeters
2 inches	5 centimeters
2½ inches	6 centimeters
4 inches	10 centimeters
5 inches	13 centimeters
6 inches	15¼ centimeters
12 inches (1 foot)	30 centimeters

metric conversion formulas

To Convert	Multiply
Ounces to grams	Ounces by 28.35
Pounds to kilograms	Pounds by .454
Teaspoons to milliliters	Teaspoons by 4.93
Tablespoons to milliliters	Tablespoons by 14.79
Fluid ounces to milliliters	Fluid ounces by 29.57
Cups to milliliters	Cups by 236.59
Cups to liters	Cups by .236
Pints to liters	Pints by .473
Quarts to liters	Quarts by .946
Gallons to liters	Gallons by 3.785
Inches to centimeters	Inches by 2.54

oven temperatures

To convert Fahrenheit to Celsius, subtract 32 from Fahrenheit, multiply the result by 5, then divide by 9.

Description	Fahrenheit	Celsius	British Gas Mark
Very cool	200°	95°	0
Very cool	225°	110°	¼
Very cool	250°	120°	½
Cool	275°	135°	1
Cool	300°	150°	2
Warm	325°	165°	3
Moderate	350°	175°	4
Moderately hot	375°	190°	5
Fairly hot	400°	200°	6
Hot	425°	220°	7
Very hot	450°	230°	8
Very hot	475°	245°	9

common ingredients and their approximate equivalents

1 cup uncooked white rice = 185 grams

1 cup all-purpose flour = 125 grams

1 stick butter (4 ounces • ½ cup • 8 tablespoons) = 115 grams

1 cup butter (8 ounces • 2 sticks • 16 tablespoons) = 225 grams

1 cup brown sugar, firmly packed = 220 grams

1 cup granulated sugar = 200 grams

Information compiled from a variety of sources, including *Recipes into Type* by Joan Whitman and Dolores Simon (Newton, MA: Biscuit Books, 1993); *The New Food Lover's Companion* by Sharon Tyler Herbst (Hauppauge, NY: Barron's, 2013); and *Rosemary Brown's Big Kitchen Instruction Book* (Kansas City, MO: Andrews McMeel, 1998).

index

Andrews McMeel Publishing
a division of Andrews McMeel Universal
1130 Walnut Street, Kansas City, Missouri 64106

www.andrewsmcmeel.com

23 24 25 26 27 SHO 10 9 8 7 6 5 4 3 2 1

ISBN: 978-1-5248-7693-7

Library of Congress Control Number: 2023931918

Photographer: Kathryn McCrary
Food Stylist: Ali Ramee
Prop Stylist: Missie Neville Crawford
Photographs by Jeremy Reper: pages ii, vi, ix, 1, 8, 21, 38, 39,
48, 55, 56, 57, 65, 93, 94, 119, 124, 132, 136, 139
Photographs by Toni Pressley: pages 83, 87

Editor: Jean Z. Lucas
Art Director: Holly Swayne
Production Editor: Elizabeth A. Garcia
Production Manager: Tamara Haus

attention: schools and businesses

Andrews McMeel books are available at quantity discounts with bulk purchase
for educational, business, or sales promotional use. For information, please e-mail the
Andrews McMeel Publishing Special Sales Department: sales@amuniversal.com.